LIFE INSURANCE AND
THE PUBLIC INTEREST

LIFE INSURANCE AND THE PUBLIC INTEREST

A Critique of Stock Company Life Insurance

by Halsey D. Josephson, C.L.U.

Crown Publishers, Inc. / New York

Contents

Introduction

An appropriate title for this book might well have been *A Plague on One of Your Houses,* since it is not an attack on the entire institution of life insurance. On the contrary, I am passionately devoted to the life insurance process as a social and financial instrument essential to the security of American families, American business, and the American economy. My target is the ownership of life insurance companies by profit-seeking stockholders, as differentiated from policyholder-owned companies called mutuals.

I shall direct my attention to these two systems, rather than to individual companies or individual managements. I concede, at the outset, that a diligent search might reveal some mutual companies less efficiently managed than some stock companies, and some stock company management teams more dedicated than some mutual management. But the *system* of stockholder-owned life insurance companies must, as I will illustrate, result in unnecessary costs to policyholders and, even more important, that system provides a fertile field for the seeds of corruption.

Effective regulation can remedy whatever is imperfect in the mutual system, for its imperfections do not include even the possibility of corruption. On the other hand, as I will point out, regulation, no matter how competent and dedicated, is impotent to contend with the vagaries of stockholder-oriented management.

While life insurance itself is vital to the public welfare, the system of stockholder-owned companies is not in the public interest.

While the fundamental incompatibility of mutual and stock companies and the awareness of the antisocial aspects of stock life insurance companies have been recognized by top officials of mutual companies for at least fifty years, indeed has been uppermost in the thoughts of many, the issue has never become explosive. The two major company associations, The American Life Convention and The Life Insurance Association of America, include both mutual and stock companies as members, some companies belonging to both associations. The membership rosters include companies that differ in age, size, locale, methods, and objectives. It is understandable that such differences do not necessarily preclude the possibility of a united front. The difference in structure, however—that is, the difference between policyholder ownership and stockholder ownership—presents an insurmountable barrier. The fundamental antagonisms may be likened to an undetonated bomb destined to explode at an undetermined time.

How is it that such incompatible philosophies have not yet come into open conflict? There are many reasons: among them are (1) there has been enough business to go around; (2) a common front has been more effective in opposing adverse legislation and regulatory infringements on "the perogatives of management"; (3) the camaraderie that has developed among the most influential high-echelon executives of both types of companies; (4) the fear of retaliation.

Perhaps, if left to their own devices, the implausible relationship would continue for years. But external forces have rather suddenly become compelling. The rapidly growing consumer movement will soon reveal to the public at large that the premiums they pay to stock life insurance companies are in excess of the cost of the coverage because of unjustifiable rewards to stockholders. The emergence of almost two thousand new stock life insurance companies over the last two decades, and the "disappearance" of so many of them, point up not only the danger of loss, but the inherent possibility of windfall profits to the investors at the expense of the policyholders. The recent passion for diversification, holding companies, and conglomerates exhibited by stock company managements has placed such pressure on the regulatory authorities that effective supervision has become virtually impossible.

It may be said that while the state insurance departments and the mutual companies have permitted stock-ownership life insurance companies to go unchallenged, an awakened public interest will shortly bring the issue to a head.

It is my objective to bring into full focus the objectionable features of stock life insurance companies and to suggest a fair and lawful procedure for their elimination.

LIFE INSURANCE AND
THE PUBLIC INTEREST

Chapter 1 *The Heart of the Problem*

Back in 1914, when the transformation of the Prudential from stockholder ownership to policyholder ownership began, the company had admitted assets of almost $323 million, and $2.5 billion of insurance in force. Incredibly, the total stockholder cash investment was a measly $91,000! By 1909, that investment had already been rewarded by $5.5 million, every penny of which came from the policyholders. The Massachusetts Insurance Commissioner said, "The stockholders have already received enrichment beyond what avarice could have dreamed of when the Company started."

To attain total mutualization, the stock was purchased and retired at a cost of $18.2 million, every cent of which, like the dividends previously paid to the stockholders, came from funds accumulated by the policyholders.[1] As a mutual company the Prudential has gone on to become the largest life insurance company in the world.[2]

Its condition, before mutualization, is a dramatic but not unique example of the way of life of established stock life insurance companies.]Money invested by stockholders plays no part in operations and is therefore superfluous; its cost unnecessarily and unreasonably drains policyholder accumulations and increases the cost of coverage; it is riskless and hence unworthy of participation in company profits.

THE BOOTLESS WASTE

Over the last hundred and twenty-five years, and particularly over the last half century, hundreds of books, many of them excellent, have described the fundamentals of life insurance in theory and practice. Being essentially textbooks and reference sources, most of them described, among many other things, the differences between mutual and stock life insurance companies, in organization, in operations, and in results. Being objective analyses, they dealt with such differences dispassionately. The writers, almost invariably, assumed the mantle of neutrality, regardless of their own beliefs.

This book has a different purpose. Believing not only that the profits to shareholders of stock life insurance companies unnecessarily and unreasonably increase the cost to policyholders, but that in addition the lure of still greater profits now threatens the wholesomeness of the institution, this writer aims at the mutualization of all existing stock companies and the prohibition of any new ones in

---

[1] Mutualization facts gleaned from:
The Life Insurance Enterprise, 1885–1910, Morton Keller.
The Private Insurance Business in the United States Economy, Nelli and Marshall.

[2] The company was incorporated under the laws of New Jersey in 1873 as The Widows' and Orphans' Friendly Society. The name was changed two years later to The Prudential Friendly Society, and in 1877 to its present name, The Prudential Insurance Company of America. It began operations in 1875. (*Best's Insurance Reports*)

America. Mutualization of stock companies is not new and, as I will show, has frequently been accomplished through fair and lawful means without loss to stockholders. My objective then is to convince the life insurance buying public and our legislators that stock-company life insurance is inimicable to the best interests of the community, is a bootless waste of policyholders' money, and is undesirable socially and economically.

This is not a revolutionary doctrine, nor is it original. Almost a century ago, Elizur Wright,[3] frequently referred to as the father of American life insurance, wrote:

> The ambition of stock subscribers and stockholders—double holders, it seems, in some cases—to manage life insurance, may be fair and proper, but it will become no less so by being better understood. To us, it does not seem wise for any legislature to farm out to capitalists the business of collecting and managing the funds provided by the people for their widows and orphans. . . . In the experimental stage of a company, which surely ought not to last many years, while the net receipts from interest are little or nothing, it is of course necessary to expend a considerable portion of the receipts from premiums in establishing the means of future business and securing an attractive nucleus of policyholders. Hence, the importance of a guarantee capital at this stage, which may quell every apprehension of a possible want of means to pay losses on the policies. But after this stage is passed, and it probably will be in two or three years, if ever, the guarantee capital becomes perfectly unnecessary, and every cent which it costs more than the earnings of its investment is a bootless extravagance and waste of the policyholders' money.

A few decades later, a New York State investigation of life insurance, known as the Armstrong Investigation, conducted by specially appointed legal counsel, Charles Evans Hughes, who later became a presidential candidate and Chief Justice of the Supreme Court of

---

[3] 1804–1885. Mathematician and actuary. Massachusetts State supervisor for insurance legislation, 1858–1866. Responsible for guarantee of cash value on lapsed policies and other nonforfeiture legislation.

the United States, included this in its report:

> In all successful life insurance companies, the capital stock soon comes to bear an insignificant relation to the resources of the company provided by its policyholders. The plan of procuring funds necessary to start the corporation through a subscription to shares is of obvious convenience at outset, but if a corporation is ever to be established upon a secure basis, it must be by a distribution of its risks over a large number of policyholders, who, whatever their formal relation to the company, have, in effect, combined in a common adventure to provide protection to all from a loss which in time is certain to fall upon each one. Without going so far as to prohibit further organization of stock corporations, it would seem to be wise not to prohibit, but rather to encourage, the formation of mutual companies upon a full legal reserve basis, provided suitable guarantees are given, of the bona fides and soundness of the enterprise.

It is conceded by all students of American life insurance that without the accomplishments and influence of Mr. Wright and the Armstrong Committee, this socially and economically essential business of life insurance would not have had the public acceptance that has been the foundation of its phenomenal growth. Their pronouncements, so much alike despite the time difference, regarding the undesirable aspects of life insurance companies owned by stockholders, must be clarified for all who wish to understand the fundamental thesis of this book. Each said in effect:

1. That guarantee capital is necessary to launch a new life insurance company.

2. That after the experimental stage has been passed, such original capital is insignificant in comparison with the resources built up by the policyholders themselves, and therefore is no longer necessary.

3. That mutual life insurance companies are more in the public interest than stock companies.

4. That profits to the capitalists who supplied the original guarantee capital are unwarranted.

16

THE NEEDS OF SOCIETY COME FIRST

The validity of the Wright and Armstrong views has been materially reinforced by almost a century of enlightened thought and legislation regarding the functions, responsibilities, dangers, and limitations of business—particularly big business. The days of the robber barons are long since gone, and it is now widely accepted that "neither the claims of ownership nor those of control can stand against the paramount interests of the community." [4] Particularly in the field of life insurance—exclusively an instrument of the people —this philosophy must prevail. "Social demands must . . . take precedence of financial motives. All [objectives] must be qualified by the overriding needs of society." [5]

Do the owners of stock in an established life insurance company contribute to the needs of society? Mr. Wright said that their investment is totally unnecessary and its cost a waste of the policyholders' money. The Armstrong Report pointed out that the capital stock bears an insignificant relation to the resources provided by the policyholders. The Prudential mutualization, and others that will be spelled out in Chapter 4, attest to the truth of these observations.

But what of those companies that remain under stockholder ownership? The invested capital averages about 1½ percent of their total admitted assets, and is just as unnecessary for continued operations as was the Prudential's $91,000. Their stockholders do not insure the policyholders. Even an elementary knowledge of premium construction makes it clear that the policyholders insure each other.

"Profits are an essential part of the corporate system. But the use of corporate power solely to serve the stockholders is no longer likely to serve the public interest." [6] It is apparent that the corporate

---

[4] *The Modern Corporation and Private Property*, Adolph A. Berle and G. C. Means.

[5] *The Purpose of Insurance Regulation*, Spencer L. Kimball.

[6] Preface by Mr. Means to the revised edition of *The Modern Corporation and Private Property*.

power of life insurance stockholders serves no one but the stockholders themselves, and the cost of the investment is a "bootless waste of the policyholders' money."

STOCK AND MUTUAL DEFINED

The late Joseph B. Maclean, in the seventh edition of his classic, *Life Insurance,* explained that there are "two kinds of life insurance companies: mutual companies which are purely cooperative associations in which the members obtain insurance at cost, whatever that may be; and stock companies, in which the policyholders are 'customers' paying a fixed price for insurance, and which are formed and financed by persons not necessarily insured in the company but who wish to make a profit from carrying on the business of life insurance."

"Stock companies have . . . a built-in profit-maker. Their mutual rivals, by definition, write only so-called participating policies. This means they are under a certain obligation to share at least some of whatever operating gains they may achieve with their policyholders in the form of dividends. Stock companies, on the other hand, can issue non-participating policies, which they almost always do. Thus, when mortality rates are down, expenses are down and investment yields are up—as has generally been true since World War II—the stockholders are the sole beneficiaries." [7]

Since virtually all of the nonparticipating insurance in force in America is in stock companies, and participating policies are sold almost exclusively by the mutuals,[8] let us turn our attention to the differences between the two kinds of life insurance coverage.

Both are issued for long durations, many covering the whole lifespan.[9] Because some may remain in force for eighty years or more,

---

[7] *Forbes Magazine,* April 15, 1964.

[8] Some participating insurance is sold by stock companies, and that subject is covered in Chapter VI.

[9] At death, the average policyholder in most companies has been insured for over thirty years.

and because the gross premium, whether participating or nonparticipating, is guaranteed and may never be increased, that premium must be based not on conditions that prevail at the inception of the contract, but on those that may develop during its continuance. The premium then must be conservatively estimated, allowing for adverse mortality experience, reduced interest returns, and increased operating costs. The margin of safety must be created regardless of whether the policy is participating or nonparticipating. The contention that nonparticipating rates are "rock bottom" is palpably fallacious. The safety margin, while smaller in nonparticipating rates, is there nonetheless. The difference is one of degree only.

All or most of the safety margin invariably proves to be unneeded. Its size is directly traceable to the expertise of company management, but we may assume that management skill is more or less equal in mutual and established stock companies. The paramount consideration for the public is not the size of the unneeded margin, but the disposition of it. Who gets it is the base issue. In the case of the mutual company, it is returned to the policyholders or, at the very least, retained for their benefit. In stock companies, it is deemed profit to the stockholders.

SOURCES OF STOCKHOLDER PROFIT

To have a clear understanding of this profit, it isn't necessary to study the various aspects of premium construction, but a simple illustration will be helpful, and perhaps even interesting. If a company were to insure a thousand people, age thirty-five, for one year, for $1,000 each, it would have to assume answers to three basic questions: How many will die during the year? What rate of interest will be earned on the premiums? How much is necessary to manage the business? If the mortality table predicts that nine will die, it will be necessary to have $9,000 on hand at the end of the year. If all premiums are payable at the beginning of the year, that figure may be discounted for interest. If 3 percent is the assumed rate, the company will need only $8,738.10 at the beginning, for that amount will grow to $9,000 by the year's end. Dividing that amount by the thousand to be insured, the premium for each will be $8.74. To this figure, perhaps 8 percent or 70 cents, must be added for operational expenses. Thus the hypothetical premium for each is $9.44.

Bear in mind that that figure results from assumptions, highly conservative assumptions, and not actual experience. Let us say that at the end of the year, analysis reveals that only seven of the insured died, that 5 percent was earned instead of 3 percent, and only 6 percent of the base premium was spent on operations. A considerable sum, about 25 percent of the premium collected, would be left over after the $7,000 in death claims was distributed. What happens to that excess, or safety margin? Stated simply, it would be returned equally to the 993 survivors and seven beneficiaries as dividends if the company was a mutual. If the policy was nonparticipating, it would go to the stockholders as profit. The issue is as simple as that. While the safety margin in the mutual company would have been greater than in a stock company, the fact remains that in the mutual company, policyholders are charged only for actual costs, while in the stock company the highly conservative assumptions (including a margin for stockholders) are pegged and permit no return to policyholders, although actual experience proves that a smaller premium would have been adequate.

Dividends paid by a mutual company reflect the actual cost of the life insurance for each year. A pegged nonparticipating rate reflects only the conservatively assumed cost at the time of issue. Quite obviously, improved medical services and new drugs lengthen the life-span. A cure for cancer, a virtual certainty some time in the future, will radically change mortality tables. But that cure, and so many others, will have no effect on the life insurance costs of a previous buyer of nonparticipating life insurance.[10] Likewise when the

---

[10] That fact is the basis of this observation in the 1970 *Shearson Institutional Report,* published by Shearson, Hammill & Co., members of the New York Stock Exchange: "Obviously, any breakthrough in the treatment of cancer or heart disease [the two principle causes of death] would be a windfall for life insurers." It would indeed be a windfall for the shareholders of stock life insurance companies. As far as mutuals are concerned, that delightful breakthrough would be a windfall only for their policyholders.

interest rate is greater than the rate assumed in the construction of the premium, the nonparticipating policyholder will continue to pay his original guaranteed premium.

This unfortunate condition may be clearly seen in the rates of the Aetna, surely a representative established stock company. In 1959, a man age thirty-five who purchased a $25,000 Whole Life nonparticipating policy in that company had a nonchanging annual premium of $556. In the years following the purchase, mortality savings and excess interest (the rate higher than the assumed rate) have resulted in decreasing costs of life insurance. Today, the Aetna will charge a thirty-five-year-old man only $417.25 [11] a year for a $25,000 Whole Life policy. That man will get the benefit of improved mortality and high interest, but the 1950 buyer will continue to pay the rate based on 1950 conditions. Contrariwise, the 1950 buyer of a participating policy will pay this year only *this year's* costs, his dividend having been increased to correspond to today's mortality and interest.

HIGHER INTEREST RATES ON POLICY LOANS?

One of the many incongruities in the mutual-stock situation is presently highlighted by the record amount of policy loans and the need for higher interest rates on such transactions.

For about three-quarters of a century, the policy loan provision has been included in life insurance contracts, with state laws setting a maximum interest rate, generally either 5 percent or 6 percent. It must be understood that reserves held by life insurance companies must be invested; in fact premiums are predicated on the assumption that the reserves will earn a specific rate, varying at different times and with different companies, between 2¼ percent and 3½ percent. Obviously, when reserves are loaned to policyholders they

---

[11] This reduced rate reflects a "discount" for size, not available to the 1950 buyer, another example of a current buyer treated more advantageously than an old one. In any event, the saving traceable to size is minor.

are not available for investment in the open market. Thus there are periods in which policy loans at 5 percent or 6 percent are more attractive than the same amount invested at a going 3 percent rate. When the going rate, however, is higher than 6 percent, as it has been during recent years, a policy loan investment represents an investment loss.

Since it has become mathematically advisable for policyholders to borrow at the guaranteed rate of 5 percent, for reinvestment at perhaps 8 percent or 9 percent, policy loans are at a record high. The companies, both mutual and stock, have been arguing for legislation permitting a higher loan rate in their contracts.

While this seems advisable, it must be remembered that the policyholders in mutual companies, through increased dividends, would be the sole beneficiaries of the interest increase, while only the stockholders in stock companies would benefit.[12] Since the states make no distinction between the two types of companies on such basic things as loan rates, it is clear that the fundamental incompatibility of the two structural setups is about to be sharpened.

LAS VEGAS WITHOUT RISK

To understand the nature of stock life insurance companies, it is necessary, first, to understand the corporate structure in general and, second, to distinguish it, in terms of its justification and its inherent risks, from the life insurance corporation.

The corporate structure is built on two groups (sometimes two functions of the same group)—the suppliers of capital, who are the risk-takers, and the managers, who exercise business judgment. The first group is rewarded, if rewards are forthcoming, purely for its risk-taking. The expression, "venture capital," means, of course, capital risked in a business enterprise or speculation. The enterprise, theoretically at least, is aimed at benefiting the community— a new means of transportation, a new product to improve health,

---

[12] Participating policyholders in stock companies would also benefit, but to a limited extent.

a faster or less costly method of production—something basic to the welfare of society that requires the investment of more capital than the promoter has at his disposal, or cares to risk. The suppliers of such capital become shareholders in the new enterprise.

The element of risk is the essential difference between the shareholders in, let us say, a manufacturing firm, and those in an established life insurance company. Seldom is the risk eliminated in the former. Such a corporation is almost certain to face the need for new capital; in fact, if it grows and prospers, the need recurs with frequency. "Over 55 percent of the growth of the large companies has been made possible by the public offering of additional securities." [13]

That such a need for additional venture capital was foreseen in the earliest days of the corporate structure is evident from "the common law that asserted that the shareholders had the sole right to invest new monies in the enterprise; and they worked this out by granting to each shareholder a preemptive right to subscribe to any additionally issued stock of the corporation." [14]

In short, the risk of the investors is not generally eliminated after initial success of the venture. The element of risk is inherent and pervading, a fact more evident in large corporations than in small ones, for expansion demands the control of greater wealth.

Regardless of size, however, a major mistake by the management of the conventional corporation can throw the whole enterprise in jeopardy. Huge sums invested in the manufacture of a useless or undesirable product, movement of the means of production to a new territory, a sudden decrease in demand after excessive production, a radical increase in the cost of raw materials and labor following the investment of huge sums in research, design, and promotion—such managerial mistakes can be catastrophic for stockholders.

Before discussing the utter absence of risk-taking and, therefore,

---

[13] *The Modern Corporation and Private Property,* Adolph A. Berle and G. C. Means.

[14] Ibid.

the lack of justification for rewards of *un*venture capital in the established life insurance corporation, let us note the one common characteristic of the successful conventional corporate enterprise and the established life insurance corporate enterprise. That characteristic is huge profits.

Among the five hundred currently most profitable corporations, Aetna Life and Casualty ranked 84th, Travelers 97th, Insurance Company of North America 148th, Lincoln National 157th, Connecticut General 159th—all exceeding in net profits such giants as Johns-Manville, Colgate-Palmolive, National Cash Register, Kaiser Industries, U.S. Gypsum, W. R. Grace, Standard Brands, Genesco, United Fruit, Reynolds Metal, and H. J. Heinz. Franklin Life ranked 362nd, exceeding Otis Elevator, R. H. Macy, Parke Davis, Dow Jones, Schenley Industries, Marshall Field, Pitney-Bowes, and others. Liberty National Life ranked 481st, ahead of such as Black & Decker, Purex, Heublein, and Hilton Hotels.[15]

All of the life insurance corporations mentioned were, of course, in the top five hundred. The next five hundred must include a considerably greater number, and the third five hundred, a still greater number. It is obvious, then, that stock life insurance companies are clearly among the nation's most profitable corporations.

In addition to the fact that the invested capital in such life insurance companies is riskless, it is as we have noted totally unnecessary. The business of those companies is to insure the lives of their policyholders, but the stockholders don't do it—*the policyholders insure each other*.

Perhaps if the invested capital in an established stock life insurance company, while not essential to operations, was subject to loss, or even risk, it could be argued that it is venture capital and therefore entitled to the customary rewards. But it is clearly riskless.[16]

---

[15] "The Dimensions Of American Business," *Forbes,* May 15, 1969. (Forbes explained that "for life insurance companies, we use net gain from operations, a figure that includes all expenses associated with new policies.")

[16] Trading in such stock, certainly not riskless, is not relevant to this discussion. The corporation is unaffected by the transfer of its stock from one person to another. The assumption must be made, in the context of this book, that the original investors, or their heirs, have retained their stock.

Unlike those of any other business in the world, costs can be reliably anticipated; even when exposed to adverse experience, quick and simple remedies are readily available. Most significant of all, however, is the fact that huge special reserves and surplus funds, *created entirely by the policyholders,* are more than adequate to counter adverse mortality and investment experience.

The hazards that face conventional business enterprises, then, are simply not evident in the operations of a life insurance company. Raw materials, machinery, even fickle public demand do not plague it. The mortality tables are practically bulletproof, and careful selection of applicants results almost invariably in mortality savings. The assumed interest rate is most often a third to a half less than the prevailing rate. And on top of it all are the policyholder-created reserves, far more than ample to meet any contingency short of the annihilation of all of us. In our capitalistic economy, it should be recognized that "if business must be able to feel free to make profits, it should not expect to be insured against losses." [17] Conversely, if investors are loss-proof, they should not be free to make profits.

NEW STOCK COMPANIES—
RISKY AND SUPERFLUOUS

New stock life insurance companies, however, while certainly incurring risk, serve no necessary or even useful purpose. They impose risk on investors, on policyholders, and on the public in general —as I will illustrate in Chapter 3. One may say that they are anti-public from their formation to their demise.

If such companies disappear, as so many have, investors and policyholders alike are losers. If they survive, they join the list of estab-

---

[17] *The Hidden Face Of Free Enterprise,* John R. Bunting.
The same thought was advanced in a recent U.S. Steel annual report, and in Clarence Randall's *A Creed for Free Enterprise.* The former said, "The American competitive enterprise system is an acknowledged profit and loss system, the hope of profits being the incentive and the fear of loss being the spur." Mr. Randall wrote, "Free enterprise means private capital, and the man who does not risk is unworthy to share the rewards."

lished stock companies, the shareholders of which are a burden borne unnecessarily by their policyholders. Their rewards, as we have seen, are a waste.

The history of new stock life insurance companies is a sad story indeed. It amply supports the contention that no new ones should be permitted.

THE INVESTMENT OF ACCUMULATED FUNDS

As we shall see, even established stock life insurance companies serve no unfulfilled public need, the mutual companies being thoroughly capable of insuring our increasing population to any desired extent. Unfortunately, the stock life insurance companies are not alone in their failure to make a significant contribution to society's needs. "The managers of many industrial firms have sought easier ways of handling the investment of their funds thereby making it possible to earn profits on investment while not advancing the productivity of many of America's basic industries." [18] This observation has direct applicability to our stock life insurance companies, presently obsessed with holding companies and various diversifications (discussed in Chapter 3). The profits on invested funds created, remember, by the policyholders are not reflected in the costs to nonparticipating policyholders and do not materially affect the costs of participating policyholders, if any. The profits inure solely to the stockholders, whose investment is unnecessary and riskless.

The waste goes on, while the company is "not advancing . . . productivity." New stock life insurance companies "have neither the capacity nor the intention of adding anything really new to the state of the art." [19] Considering the nature of the life insurance business, even established companies with capable management have extremely little to add.

---

[18] *Our Depleted Society*, Seymour Melman.

[19] Equity Research Associate's Report, October 15, 1964.

In connection with "the investment of their funds," it is revealing to note that in the present tragic struggles of the casualty companies, particularly those heavily engaged in automobile coverage, management argues that investment income should not be considered relevant to the cost structure. Stock insurance companies quite obviously believe that the funds created by the policyholders, and the profits they produce, are the possessions of the stockholders and so have nothing whatever to do with policyholder costs. I find this view incompatible with an enlightened philosophy of the social obligations of American business.

Chapter 2 How the Policyholders Come Out

An understanding of the basic differences between mutual and stock life insurance companies doesn't necessarily give a reader, or a prospective buyer, a clear picture of how stockholder rewards affect his life insurance premiums. It is natural for him to ask, "Specifically, what shall I be called upon to pay for a similar policy in each of the two types of companies?" The purpose of this chapter is to answer that question.

Comparisons depend, of course, on the size of the dividends paid by the mutuals.[20] (The nonparticipating premium of the stock com-

---

[20] The impact of dividends on participating policies is dramatically revealed in the 1970 experience of the New York Life Insurance Company. As of June of that year, 170,000 policyholders were receiving annual dividends in *excess* of their premiums. Instead of paying on their premium due dates, they were receiving. Many of them, finding their good fortune incredible, wrote to the New York Life

pany is pegged and not subject to fluctuations.) Since the dividends depend on the experience each year of the issuing companies, they cannot be guaranteed. There are, however, two reliable ways of measuring their size, both of which are readily available to every agent, and hence to every prospective buyer. The first is called the Actual History Basis. This shows the amounts actually paid over a given period in the past on a similar policy. Thus the prospective buyer learns exactly what a man of his age paid who bought the same policy ten, twenty, or thirty years ago.

The second method is called Projection of Current Scale. It predicts the size of the dividends the new buyer will get if the formula presently in use is continued. This means that a prospective buyer, age thirty-five, will receive at the end of his first year exactly the amount refunded currently to a man who bought his policy a year before, when he was thirty-five. And it means that he will receive at the end of his fifth year exactly the amount refunded currently to a man who purchased his policy five years ago when he was thirty-five. There is no magic or guesswork involved in the projection method. It is simply the extension of a current actuality.

Certainly, comparing costs to a policyholder of participating and nonparticipating policies on *both* bases should be revealing, particularly when measured over significant periods of time. And that is precisely what I shall do on the following pages.

Method No. I: Actual History Basis

The chart that follows shows exactly what a thirty-five-year-old buyer, who bought $10,000 Whole Life policies from the partici-

---

in the belief that errors had been made! A total of 600,000 policyholders were receiving dividends in excess of 75 percent of their premiums. Approximately 1,440,000 insureds, 98.6 percent of all insured in 1953 or earlier, were receiving 1970 dividends that exceeded 50 percent of their annual premiums.

It is likely that similar records have been compiled by other mutual companies, proportionate to their size. While all this has been going on, nonparticipating policyholders of stock companies continue to pay the same premium they started with, notwithstanding record-breaking interest rates and mortality savings traceable to wonder drugs and fantastic lifesaving surgical techniques. No wonder then that shareholders in stock life insurance companies have a risk-proof investment.

pating Northwestern Mutual and the nonparticipating Connecticut
General back in 1935, has paid for each in all the years since his
purchases.

Year	Age	Northwestern Mutual Net Premium	Connecticut General Nonpar Premium
1935	35	$268.80	$208.20
1936	36	198.00	208.20
1937	37	206.90	208.20
1938	38	200.10	208.20
1939	39	199.20	208.20
1940	40	198.40	208.20
1941	41	191.00	208.20
1942	42	189.70	208.20
1943	43	188.50	208.20
1944	44	188.80	208.20
1945	45	187.80	208.20
1946	46	185.00	208.20
1947	47	185.10	208.20
1948	48	185.20	208.20
1949	49	206.30	208.20
1950	50	207.20	208.20
1951	51	207.90	208.20
1952	52	205.90	208.20
1953	53	204.20	208.20
1954	54	201.50	208.20
1955	55	187.70	208.20
1956	56	185.70	208.20
1957	57	185.00	208.20
1958	58	170.90	208.20
1959	59	165.30	208.20
1960	60	157.10	208.20

Year	Age	Northwestern Mutual Net Premium	Connecticut General Nonpar Premium
1961	61	153.60	208.20
1962	62	148.50	208.20
1963	63	146.10	208.20
1964	64	125.70	208.20
1965	65	121.90	208.20
1966	66	101.40	208.20
1967	67	97.40	208.20
1968	68	73.30	208.20
1969	69	68.80	208.20
1970	70	64.20	208.20

The buyer paid a total of $6,158.20 to the Northwestern Mutual, and $7,287 to the Connecticut General—a difference of more than 11 percent of the face amount, or death benefit. The fact that in 1970 his guaranteed cash value on his participating policy is more than $200 in excess of the cash value on his nonparticipating policy is noteworthy, but almost immaterial compared with the differences in premium payments. Note that only in the first year, back in 1935, was the nonparticipating premium less than the Northwestern Mutual premium. In every year since, the dividend on his participating policy was more than sufficient to bring his premium to the Northwestern under his payment to the Connecticut General.

A BROADER COMPARISON

Since my conclusions are based on differences in systems rather than differences between companies, some may argue that my comparison is too limited to be meaningful. Actually, the two companies are acknowledged leaders in their respective fields. Nevertheless, I will make the same kind of comparison, based on averaging the costs of three companies in each category for varying periods.

The two charts that follow compare the average premiums paid to three representative mutual companies—Connecticut Mutual, New York Life, and Northwestern Mutual—and three representative stock companies—Aetna, Connecticut General,[21] and Equitable of Iowa—on $10,000 Whole Life policies, issued to men aged thirty-five, in 1945 and in 1950. Bear in mind that the premiums listed are the *actual* amounts paid in each year under consideration.

POLICIES ISSUED IN 1945

Year	Average of Three Stock Companies	Average of Three Mutual Companies
1	$222.03	$271.13
2	222.03	228.80
3	222.03	221.37
4	222.03	210.87
5	222.03	209.00
6	222.03	207.43
7	222.03	205.37
8	222.03	204.33

[21] To avoid misunderstanding of the corporate structures of Aetna and Connecticut General, the relationship of the two should be made clear at the outset.

By an exchange of stock offer early in 1962, the Connecticut General Life Insurance Company acquired more than 98 percent of the outstanding stock of Aetna Insurance Company. Under the offer, shareholders of Aetna received 1.2 shares of Connecticut General's new $5 par value stock for each Aetna share.

In connection with a corporate reorganization in late 1964 Aetna Life offered 1.9 shares of its stock for the minority interest outstanding in the Aetna Casualty and Surety Company.

On December 29, 1967, a reorganization of the corporate structure of Aetna Life and affiliates became effective. All shares of Aetna Life were exchanged, on a share for share basis, for shares of Aetna Life and Casualty Company established in 1967. The new parent is licensed as a property and casualty company and now holds all the outstanding shares of Aetna Life, Aetna Casualty and Surety, and Standard Fire.

Year	Average of Three Stock Companies	Average of Three Mutual Companies
9	222.03	200.27
10	222.03	198.50
11	222.03	180.67
12	222.03	192.47
13	222.03	191.37
14	222.03	183.53
15	222.03	173.70
16	222.03	141.13
17	222.03	169.93
18	222.03	168.00
19	222.03	158.30
20	222.03	136.63
21	222.03	64.60
22	222.03	118.87
23	222.03	110.77
24	222.03	98.27
25	222.03	94.70

POLICIES ISSUED IN 1950

Year	Average of Three Stock Companies	Average of Three Mutual Companies
1	$229.43	$279.07
2	229.43	246.10
3	229.43	229.97
4	229.43	225.63
5	229.43	220.57
6	229.43	211.27

Year	Average of Three Stock Companies	Average of Three Mutual Companies
7	229.43	205.43
8	229.43	199.50
9	229.43	194.87
10	229.43	189.47
11	229.43	183.20
12	229.43	176.00
13	229.43	171.07
14	229.43	158.47
15	229.43	148.97
16	229.43	143.00
17	229.43	129.33
18	229.43	120.07
19	229.43	106.33
20	229.43	100.27

These actual histories provide conclusive evidence that mutual life insurance is superior to nonparticipating stock company coverage. But let us go further and make similar comparisons on the second method.

Method No. 2—Projection of Current Dividend Scales

The following comparison illustrates twenty year results on $10,000 Whole Life policies issued currently to men age thirty-five by the nonparticipating Aetna and the participating Connecticut Mutual. The nonparticipating premium is, of course, pegged. The participating premiums reflect dividend payments based on a projection of the 1970 dividend scale—currently an actuality.

Aetna		Connecticut Mutual
$ 186.10	Gross Premium	$ 218.50
186.10	Average Annual Net Premium—	148.30
	20 years	
3762.00	Total Premiums paid—20 years	2966.40
3420.00	20th Year Cash Value	3420.70
(Cost) 342.00	20th Year Net Results	(Gain) 454.30

Here again the contention may be made that I have handpicked companies, and further that a comparison of individual companies does not provide conclusive evidence that a participating mutual policy is superior to a nonparticipating stock company policy. Despite the fact that such a contention is invalid, since the two Hartford companies are acknowledged leaders in their fields, I will illustrate the differences based on averaging three mutuals—Connecticut Mutual, New York Life, and Northwestern Mutual—against the average of the three stock companies—Aetna, Connecticut General, and Equitable of Iowa—on the same basis.

Average of Three Stock Nonparticipating Policies		*Average of Three Mutual Participating Policies*
$ 186.33	Gross Annual Premium	$ 229.03
186.33	Annual Net Premium	154.57
	over 20 Years	
3,727.00	Total 20 net premiums	3,090.90
3,393.33	20th year cash value	3,534.00
(Cost) 333.66	20th year result	(Gain) 493.13

How about Participating Policies Issued by Stock Companies?

In spite of the fact that "stock company" is almost synonymous with "nonparticipating," most of the established stock companies issue participating contracts in addition to their basic nonpar policies. The background of this anomaly will be spelled out in Chapter 6, and you will see that, unlike nonparticipating coverage that donates the entire unused safety margin in the premiums to the stockholders, the margin in participating insurance is divided (in curious ways) between the policyholders and the stockholders. Naturally then, the participating policyholder in a stock company, no matter how small his portion of the unused safety margin, fares better than his nonparticipating counterpart, and a comparison between participating policyholders in stock and mutual companies shows a smaller advantage to the mutual buyer. The advantage, however, is still clearly with the latter.

THE TWO METHODS AGAIN

The three charts that follow are based on actual histories. They compare the average net premiums actually paid on $10,000 Whole Life policies, in the three stock companies—Aetna, Connecticut General, and Equitable of Iowa—and the three mutuals, Connecticut Mutual, New York Life, and Northwestern Mutual, by men age thirty-five who bought their policies in 1935, 1945, and 1950.

PURCHASED IN 1935

Year	Average of Three Stock Companies	Average of Three Mutual Companies
1	$255.77	$271.13
2	216.20	234.07
3	215.30	216.77
4	209.63	212.53
5	209.77	210.57
6	209.33	209.23

Year	Average of Three Stock Companies	Average of Three Mutual Companies
7	208.80	207.00
8	210.07	209.83
9	211.47	210.60
10	211.27	209.97
11	211.10	193.73
12	212.53	205.73
13	212.47	205.40
14	222.80	211.60
15	224.57	209.63
16	224.20	178.30
17	224.20	208.97
18	223.67	207.30
19	222.00	204.63
20	221.63	200.33
21	219.57	127.03
22	215.10	187.47
23	212.37	185.03
24	206.73	176.13
25	205.17	171.57
26	200.73	161.23
27	197.43	154.63
28	196.23	150.77
29	189.23	139.50
30	186.50	121.43
31	185.00	114.60
32	183.60	96.43
33	165.70	83.27
34	151.63	64.87
35	123.10	58.73

PURCHASED IN 1945

Year	Average of Three Stock Companies	Average of Three Mutual Companies
1	$275.73	$271.13
2	230.17	228.80
3	229.23	211.37
4	224.20	210.87
5	221.27	209.00
6	218.27	207.43
7	217.93	205.37
8	215.67	204.33
9	213.00	200.27
10	210.73	198.50
11	206.90	180.67
12	201.90	192.47
13	201.23	191.37
14	195.37	183.53
15	194.17	173.70
16	190.50	141.13
17	188.13	169.93
18	186.10	168.00
19	180.70	158.30
20	176.80	136.63
21	175.10	64.60
22	165.43	118.87
23	158.57	110.77
24	149.47	98.27
25	127.13	94.70

PURCHASED IN 1950

Year	Average of Three Stock Companies	Average of Three Mutual Companies
1	$278.77	$279.07
2	251.23	246.10
3	237.27	229.97
4	232.60	225.63
5	227.43	220.57
6	220.20	211.27
7	214.80	205.43
8	211.50	199.50
9	206.50	194.87
10	202.57	189.47
11	198.33	183.20
12	193.60	176.00
13	190.60	171.07
14	184.80	158.47
15	179.60	148.97
16	176.27	143.00
17	172.90	129.33
18	162.30	120.07
19	156.37	106.33
20	145.17	100.27

Method No. 2—Projections of Current Dividend Scales

Now let us see the same kind of comparison—participating policies in both types of companies—based on projecting current (1970) scales. Here again the figures average the same three companies in each category.

Average of Three Stock Companies		*Average of Three Mutual Companies*
$ 232.57	Gross Annual Premium	$ 229.03
171.97	Annual Net Premium over 20 years	154.57
3,474.23	Total 20 Net Premiums	3,090.90
3,650.07	20th Year Cash Value	3,534.00
175.84	Net Gain Over Cost	443.10

The Total Picture

Clearly, these comparisons, based on the two established methods, for varying durations, reveal the superiority of participating policies issued by mutual companies. How could the results be otherwise when the unused safety margins in the mutual policies go entirely to the benefit of policyholders, while in the stock companies they pass entirely, or in part, to the stockholders?

In regard to cost measurements, there has been, during the last few years, considerable criticism both from inside and outside the life insurance business of the traditional net cost method. This method simply adds up the premiums paid during a given period, generally twenty years, and then subtracts the cash value available at the end of the period plus the total of dividends paid, if any. The difference has been called "the net cost."

The chief criticism of this measurement is that it disregards interest. It equates a dollar paid at the end of the chosen period with one paid at the beginning. Moreover, it disregards "negative" interest, that is interest lost by virtue of higher premiums in the early years. There has been other criticism far too esoteric for this discussion.

In response to the shortcomings of the traditional net cost measurement, The National Underwriter Company published in late 1969 "Cost Facts On Life Insurance," a series of compilations

41

based on more sophisticated standards. The project was reviewed by Dr. Joseph M. Belth, professor of insurance in the Graduate School of Business at Indiana University and a learned and articulate commentator on various aspects of life insurance, in the September 1970 issue of *The Journal of Risk and Insurance*. Despite some criticism, he concluded that the new volume "provides far better life insurance price information than has heretofore been available."

One of its calculations, which took into account interest rates, mortality rates, and lapse rates, none of which influences the traditional net cost results, was chosen by Dr. Belth for illustrative purposes. In chart form, he presented the "new" costs, based on $25,000 Whole Life policies, issued at various ages, by thirty-eight established companies selling participating policies, and sixteen companies selling nonparticipating policies.

These new measurements simply substantiate the facts that nonparticipating policies are the most costly and that participating policies issued by mutual companies are less costly than participating policies issued by stock companies.

The new cost measurement is undoubtedly more sophisticated, but in general the relative standings remain the same.

This conclusion was reached by Robert B. Mitchell, former editor of *The National Underwriter* (a publication of the National Underwriter Company), in his article "What Sophisticated Formulas Do to Policy Cost Ranking." After analyzing the methods illustrated in "Cost Facts On Life Insurance," Mr. Mitchell asked, "What may we expect in the way of results from easy availability of these sophisticated figures for measuring life insurance net costs, and comparing one company with others?" He answered the question with this observation: "I doubt that they will prove very upsetting to the business. Most of the companies that looked good enough on the traditional basis so that their agents stress cost in selling will continue to look good." [22]

---

[22] *The National Underwriter,* November 15, 1969.

Chapter 3 *Seeds of Corruption*

THE FIRST RED LIGHT

The owners of shares of stock in a life insurance company have the same motivations and expectations as those who own stock in any commercial enterprise. Indeed, they doubtless own stock in some of those enterprises themselves, and they view their total holdings in terms of income or growth or both. They see nothing special in the life insurance process, and so long as ownership in such an endeavor is permissible, they shouldn't be expected to. After all, they don't invest to suffer a loss, or to come out even when they are moved to sell.

In turn, the managers of such life insurance companies, frequently shareholders themselves, have the same financial aspirations. These desires are evident regardless of the age of the company, although, in theory at least, the stockholders and managers of an established company have more modest hopes than do the windfall-seeking backers and managers of new companies.

Entrepreneurial zeal may be a boon to many businesses, but to life insurance it is a source of danger, mainly because the stock life insurance system not only permits questionable practices, but actually encourages them.

Diversification and speculation—the red lights presently flashing —are inimical to the life insurance process, from its actuarial precision to its fiduciary obligations.

The applicability of the word "pollute" is not limited to air and water. As defined in Webster's, it means "to render ceremonially or morally impure; impairs the purity of; destroy or violate the sanctity of." The verb may be applied to the actions of many stock life insurance companies in regard to the life insurance process and to the institution generally.

Let us turn our attention first to the holding company device, the instrument of diversification, and then to new stock company formations, so frequently motivated by the lure of huge profits.

The holding company device, adopted by many stock life insurance companies, creates a new parent company of which the original company becomes a subsidiary. Most frequently, this is accomplished by an exchange of shares in the insurance company for shares in the holding company. Far less often, the original company changes its corporate purpose and places its entire insurance operation in a wholly owned insurance subsidiary. Regardless of how it is accomplished, the stock life insurance company, instead of being owned by its stockholders, becomes the possession of the shareholders of the holding company.

It is not a new stock life insurance company development,[23] but the last five or six years have produced a virtual epidemic of them.

---

[23] In the 1930s, a holding company that held the majority of a life insurer's stock suddenly failed, causing a severe financial crisis in the insurance company. The holding company had been guilty of manipulating the assets of the insurance corporation. ("Motivations Underlying the Mutualization of Stock Life Insurance Companies," Linda Pickthorne Fletcher, *The Journal of Risk and Insurance,* March, 1966.)

The motivations for the transactions are both interesting and frightening.

"While few in top management positions will admit it publicly, one of the major reasons for holding company formations is to minimize, if not eliminate, the stringent insurance regulations which now restrict them in the interests of policyholder protection." [24]

Far more ingenuous is this explanation by Edward J. Falls, vice-president, counsel, and secretary of Beneficial Standard Life Insurance Company: [25]

> There must be something to this holding company approach, because a lot of people in a lot of states representing a lot of money invested in major insurance companies have decided that the long range fate of their company depends upon its ability to make investments in competition with the prudent business world and not as restricted—perhaps unnecessarily in their special case—by the inflexible provisions of the insurance codes of the several states.
>
> . . . assume that we have formed [a holding company] and acquired 95 per cent of the stock of X Insurance Company. What does the picture look like? Well, let's say X Insurance Company stock prior to the exchange was worth $100 million. The holding company thus owns stock having a value of $95 million.
>
> Now some will quarrel with me about whether or not this exact valuation transfers itself to the holding company. Let's be conservative and book 95 per cent of the stock as an asset of the holding company to be worth $50 million.
>
> "But," you cry, "to what avail? This is the only thing that this poor, underprivileged new company owns."
>
> Not on your tintype, gentlemen! It owns the right to use that stock as collateral to borrow equity capital. It owns the right to make investments in competition with similarly situated and similarly capitalized business enterprises.
>
> It owns the right to operate its investments under the regulation of the SEC or general law of the state—the same laws applicable to the people with whom it is competing for yield. It owns a charter

---

[24] "Management Today," Thomas C. Laughlin and Daniel P. Kedzie, *Best's Review,* April 1970.

[25] *Insuranceflash,* December 1968.

which enables it to acquire subsidiary companies in all fields of endeavor—the only test being whether or not management believes the acquisitions will be of value.

Obviously, all these things are based upon leverage capital. But didn't we just agree that there is nothing wrong with using your credit?

Stripping the transaction to its essentials, it is merely an exercise in leverage whereby the true value of the insurance company's assets are freed to be utilized by investment management.

I do not believe, as has been alleged, that this is a "getting out from under insurance regulation" approach to corporate investment.

Others, however, believe the holding company *is* a mechanism for "getting out from under insurance regulation." Orville F. Grahame, vice-president and general counsel of Paul Revere Corporation, made this clear when he said: [26]

Holding companies, because they are not subject to the investment restrictions unique to the insurance business, can compete with other financial institutions for capital on an equal footing.

Newsday, July 8, 1970, claimed that "the formation of holding companies and subsidiaries has allowed the life insurance industry to skirt state regulatory control in many areas. Because life insurance is a mutual venture, it has been governed by a separate and special set of laws to protect policyholder interests. Holding companies can be a device to circumvent those separate and special laws."

WHAT DO THE REGULATORS THINK?

More authoritative, and certainly more revealing, are these observations of New York State Insurance Superintendent Richard E. Stewart: [27]

[26] An address at a meeting of the Worcester (Mass.) Insurance Society, reported in *The National Underwriter*, January 11, 1969.

[27] A talk before the insurance section of the American Bar Association, reported in *The National Underwriter*, August 23, 1969.

At first, holding companies were a way of making it easier to do an active insurance business.

A life insurer wanted access to the market in a state, but did not want to shape its entire operation to that state's laws, and so it planted a local subsidiary.[28]

These examples suggest why the holding company has, in the past, not been much of a problem to insurance regulation. First, it was in the hands of people who wanted to do an insurance business, and regulation presupposes that the people in the regulated business want to be there. Second, while in these examples the holding company was often used to evade the spirit of regulatory laws, it served as a safety valve for the release of economic forces that would have broken through in any event.

A few years ago, the dominant motive for forming holding companies changed. The impetus still came from within the insurance business, but the new motive was not to facilitate the doing of that business. On the contrary, it was to diversify away from the conventional insurance enterprise.

The goal in this second phase of the insurance holding company was flexibility, real or imagined. It coincided with the rise to top management of many companies, for the first time, of men whose background was not in sales or underwriting, but in investment.

---

[28] The formation of holding companies is, unfortunately, not the only available method of evading strict state requirements. A favorite, particularly in New York State, the most demanding of all, is to form a subsidiary, or buy out a small New York State licensed company and thus obtain access to the New York market while remaining free of that state's requirements and restrictions. A prime example, among many, was the formation of Lincoln National of New York by the Lincoln National of Indiana.

It is interesting to note that New York State imposes a tight restriction on sales commissions and applies that restriction to all companies it licenses, regardless of far greater permissiveness of other states in which they operate. It is common for stock companies, not licensed in New York, to pay commissions almost double the rate allowed in that state. (Such fat commissions may be necessary to attract agents to sell their high-priced policies.) The formation of a New York subsidiary does not prohibit the parent company, operating perhaps in all the other forty-nine states, from paying sales commissions far in excess of New York's limit.

Newsday, in its July 1970 life insurance articles, underscored this method. It said, ". . . many companies avoid New York control by forming subsidiaries that operate only in New York. The parent corporation can then avoid New York regulations." This device is employed exclusively by stock companies. I am not aware of its use by a single mutual company.

These men wanted to use the resources of their insurance companies—to achieve more profit and honor than they foresaw in the conventional insurance enterprise.

In this second phase, the new motives for forming holding companies are the key to the new concern of the regulators. First, managements wanted to move money and talent away from the classical insurance business, to wander off from their entailed duty station. Thereby they subtly affronted the pride of the regulators and openly defied the presumptive constancy of regulatory law.

The invasion was resisted by insurer managements because it presented a direct threat to their prestige and even their tenure, and because the invasion was mounted upon the insulting ground that scientific management from outside could make insurer assets yield more than could seasoned insurer managements. The regulators resisted the invasion partly because they were mobilized by the industry and partly because they feared, not without reason, that the integration of insurance with unregulated business and the dominance of general entrepreneurial values over the traditions of insurance would place heavy strain on the established regulatory system.

For the moment, the public, the industry and the regulators are bewitched by the vivid and understandable—the drama of take-overs, the legerdemain of growth by acquisition, the daredevilry of leverage, and the barbarities of corporate plunder. But what now fascinates us most is least likely to endure. Regulation can, should, and doubtless will bring under control the zanier antisocial proclivities of the insurance holding company.

A special study in New York concluded that conduct within such a holding company structure could be regulated, and probably at the state level, if government kept insurer diversification within limits and concentrated regulatory energy on the points of contact between insurers and their noninsurance affiliates, where abuses such as milking and conflict of interest can best be identified, quantified, and subjected to familiar regulatory techniques.

DID SOMEONE MENTION WALL STREET?

Regardless of whether the New York Law "will bring under control the zanier antisocial proclivities of the insurance holding company" (I think it is too permissive), it is enlightening to explore some of the financial maneuverings that brought it about.

I don't mean that anything that was done was illegal. But I wish to present what I regard as an excessive interest in investment lures and stock prices—attractions which, in the context of this book, belong exclusively to stock insurance companies.

"The holding company made it possible to utilize capital more effectively by dividing upstream excess capital or 'surplus surplus' " [29] (Congressman Emanuel Celler, chairman of the House Committee on the Judiciary has been quoted as saying that the "surplus surplus" is, in fact, a trust fund for policyholders which would be put to good use if applied to reduce premiums.) [30] As a prime example, the Great American Insurance Company passed on a dividend of $172 million to its holding company parent in January 1969. This amount was three times the size of the parent company's assets before the acquisition. On September 9, 1970, Great American and the Constellation Reinsurance Company, one of its subsidiaries, were charged in a citation by the New York State Insurance Department with violating the investment and holding company provisions of the New York Insurance Law, according to *The New York Times,* September 10, 1970. The issues have not yet come to trial.

However, on December 3, 1970, the largest fine ever imposed by the New York State Insurance Department—$100,000—was levied against Great American Insurance Company. Its subsidiary, Constellation Reinsurance Corporation, was also fined.

The Wall Street Journal, in reporting the story on December 4, said, "Great American is more than 99% owned by National General Corp., a West Coast conglomerate with interests in theaters, movie and television production, book publishing and savings and loan associations, as well as insurance." A life insurance company, Great American Life Insurance Company of East Orange, New Jersey, is one of the entities in the conglomerate.

The New York State Superintendent of Insurance, Richard E.

---

[29] "Revolutionary Changes," William W. Amos, Vice President of Research for the First Boston Corporation, *The Spectator,* April 1970.

[30] George F. Reed, Pennsylvania Insurance Commissioner, March 19, 1970.

Stewart, in announcing the record fine, said, "The department will keep under continuing review the conduct of Great American and its affiliates to determine whether further action, such as removal from office of certain directors of Great American Insurance Co. is necessary to protect policyholders, insurance consumers and the general public from unlawful and improper conduct."

The Wall Street Journal reported in its story that "it's known that the Securities and Exchange Commission for nearly a year has been investigating the circumstances surrounding [Great American's] fight to acquire Armour & Co. . . . The result of the investigation is a lengthy analysis, currently in draft form, that may be included in the SEC's report to Congress on the effect of institutional investors on the stock market." Additional details of the National General–Great American relationship will be found on pages 66–68.

Far less sensational was this item in the 1969 Annual Report of the BMA Corporation, a holding company, owning among others, the Business Men's Assurance Company: "In October of 1969, the Board of Directors of Business Men's Assurance Company declared a special cash dividend of $18,000,000. As 99.8% of Business Men's Assurance Company's stock is held by BMA Corporation,[31] the net effect was a transfer of funds to the Corporation. . . . Although this transfer had no effect on the consolidated statement of the Corporation, total assets of Business Men's Assurance Company were reduced."

The 1969 Report, in explaining the operations of the insurance company, stated, "The asset and surplus structures of Business Men's Assurance Company were altered by a special cash dividend of $18,000,000," which accounted entirely for the reduction of that company's unassigned surplus from $52 million (figures rounded off to the nearest million) at the end of 1968 to $39 million at the end of 1969. Had the special cash dividend not been declared the unassigned surplus at the end of 1969 would have been $57 million.

The entire issued capital stock of Business Men's Assurance

---

[31] This holding company owns the BMA Real Estate Corporation, a development organization with twenty-five projects underway in early 1970; the BMA Securities Corporation dealing in equity products; and is hopeful of acquiring the O'Meara-Chandler Corporation of Houston, Texas, a construction and development company.

Company consists of six million shares at $2.00 par value per share of $12 million. Total assets of the company, *after* payment of the $18 million special dividend, were $348 million at the end of 1969, of which $265 million constituted policy reserves. The policyholders, whose premiums created those reserves and substantially all of the unassigned surplus, as well, did not vote on the $18 million special cash dividend.

"The holding firms not only expand the insurance companies' influence over the economy but also pose a threat to the safety of policyholders' money. There have already been cases where parent holding companies have extracted life insurance funds for their own use." [32]

At least a partial explanation of such financial transactions was provided by John R. Beckett, president of Transamerica Corporation, owner of Occidental Life of California, who was quoted as having said that they result largely from the demand of stockholders.[33]

The reactions of investors to the movement of insurance companies into holding companies has been "generally favorable" according to William W. Amos.[34] But my favorite official observation was made by John T. Gurash, executive vice-president of Insurance Company of North America (INA) in an interview by the *Spectator* editor, published in the April 1969 issue. Mr. Gurash said, "After some thirty years in the insurance business during which I have been concerned with premiums, losses, expenses, the nitty gritty of insurance, I am now rather surprised to find myself worrying more about what is happening on Wall Street than what is happening in the insurance marketplace."

JUST A FEW ABUSES

The New York Insurance Department, traditionally the most effective of all state insurance departments, appointed a special com-

---

[32] *Newsday,* July 8, 1970.

[33] *The National Underwriter,* January 11, 1969.

[34] "Revolutionary Changes," *The Spectator,* April 1970.

mittee on April 28, 1967, to report on insurance holding companies. Its report, to which I previously referred, suggested restrictions, particularly in regard to noninsurance control over insurance companies. Preliminary to its report, it sent a questionnaire to the insurance commissioners of all states, The District of Columbia, Guam, Puerto Rico, and the Virgin Islands. Thirty-five responses were received, reporting regulatory problems with domestic insurance companies, which arose from intercorporate transactions among affiliated insurance and noninsurance corporations; the control of insurance companies by holding companies; and concern regarding the integrity of holding company management. Twenty-three actual abuses were cited. The dozen that follow, clearly point up the dangers.[35]

> "Problems involving transferring of assets between holding company and insurance subsidiary."
>
> "Substitution of assets, i.e. admitted assets vs. non-admitted assets; e.g., accounts receivable substituted for securities."
>
> "Problems arise from a tendency to obscure the value of assets passing from one corporation to another."
>
> "Donation of real estate by parent insurer to subsidiary insurer where costs of maintenance exceed income."
>
> "The holding company pledged assets belonging to the insurance company to secure an obligation of the parent corporation."
>
> "Entries concerning non-insurance transactions shown as amounts due from affiliates creating a false or misleading asset."
>
> "Assets of the insurance company were siphoned off by the holding company and used to form other companies—premium finance and motor bike sales."
>
> "Some of the liabilities of the young life companies have been assumed by their holding companies thereby giving the life companies the appearance of being profit-making concerns prematurely."

---

[35] These summary outlines were quoted in the New York Committee report.

"Problems involving—payment by insurance company of holding company expenses."

"Intercompany transactions and intermingling of records and books of account making a determination of true financial condition difficult and impeding the progress of an examination."

"The Department of Insurance is unable to ascertain who controls these insurance holding companies."

"Several insurers now in liquidation engaged in such [intercorporate transactions] with resulting loss to policyholders. Some were so-called management contracts."

After such a list, can anyone ignore the red lights flashing around the holding company proliferation? Of course, the Special Committee did not ignore them. In its report, it said, and Governor Rockefeller subsequently quoted in his message to the New York Legislature:

While holding companies are not themselves new, the dominant motives for their formation may be changing from a desire to facilitate the conduct of the insurance business to a desire to shift away from the insurance business and to subordinate insurance to other business objectives. This change in motive will increase the strain on the established regulatory system.

Further, the opportunities for pyramiding and excessive accumulation of economic power through the use of holding companies are real and potentially contrary to the public interest. When a noninsurance holding company system includes an insurance company within it, its potential for specific harm becomes greater since tempting reservoirs of liquid assets become accessible to persons without an appreciation of the security needs of the insurance enterprise, and the interests of the policyholders thus become vulnerable.

Charles D. Mathews, member of the Texas Insurance Board said, in September 1970, "A major problem facing the insurance regulator today, and a problem growing by leaps and bounds as the regulator looks to the future, is the problem of the holding company.

"If you will study the failure of insurance companies in Texas over the period of the last twenty years, you will find, almost without exception, that with each failure a holding company has been somehow involved. Today we have no power to regulate holding companies in their relation to the field of insurance. A holding company with stock untraded on the market and with no means of establishing a fair cash market value can acquire control of a sound and financially responsible insurance company, and milk it dry— and we have to sit idly by without power to prevent such action."

All sorts of reasons, explanations, and rationalizations have been advanced for the proliferation of holding companies, whether insurance or noninsurance controlled, but basic to the entire movement were the greed of stockholders and the desire of management to satisfy it, and, secondarily, the restlessness and unbridled ambition of management.

It may be argued that greater freedom of investment of life insurance funds had become advisable, that the doors should have been opened wider for equity investments. But it is obvious that such permissiveness could have been won without recourse to devious stock manipulations. It has been contended (without merit, I feel certain) that the public was "demanding one-stop financial services" from life insurance companies. Basically, this referred to a real or imagined public interest in a "balance" between guaranteed-dollar and equity-dollar investments, as opposed to the traditional fixed-dollar benefits of life insurance. The mechanism to accomplish this was simply a division of policyholder payments into life insurance premiums and mutual fund share purchases. In the annuity field, it was simply the introduction of a variable (based on common stock fluctuations) as an alternate to the traditional guaranteed annuity. But these things could have been, and indeed were, made available without holding companies, conglomerates, and such devices, so inimical to traditional and sound life insurance practices.

Instead of the simple readjustments to the reality of inflation, if adjustments *within* the life insurance structure were deemed responsive to "public demand" and "consumer-orientation," we witnessed a long series of radical departures from sound and proven life insurance operations.

WHO OWNS WHAT?

The entire list of diversifications would probably require more pages than this book contains. The following are sufficient for an understanding of the developments (*see* Appendix A for more examples):

The Continental Assurance Company and Continental Casualty of Chicago, formed the CNA Financial Corporation, a holding company, in late 1967. The holding company has since acquired Tsai Management and Research Corporation (mutual funds and other investments); The General Finance Corporation (consumer and automobile loan firm); Larwin Group Companies (a network of companies operating in home building, mortgage servicing, commercial development, etc.); an 81 percent voting interest in CNA Nuclear Leasing, Inc., and Kane Financial Corporation (real estate, medical and dental supplies, and nursing homes). In addition, the holding company formed CNA Realty Corporation; established CNA Investor Services, Inc., as a broker-dealer; and CNA Hotel & Leisure, Inc.[36] (During the preparation of this manuscript, the *New York Times* reported on August 22, 1970: "Diners' Club, Inc., the big credit card company that this week reported a loss of $29.1-million for the fiscal year ended March 31, has negotiated a $150-million refinancing of its bank debt—but only after the Continental Corporation, the giant insurance holding company that owns 88 per cent of its stock, guaranteed repayment of the loan.")

Aetna Life and Casualty Company, through its holding company, entered the land-development field in a joint venture with the Kaiser Aluminum and Chemical Corporation, in addition to its acquisitions in the mutual fund and variable annuity fields.

---

[36] Robert M. Powell in the *Spectator*, April 1970.

The holding company of the Travelers has acquired interests in real estate and mineral concerns through the Prospect Company, a subsidiary of its Travelers Equities Fund, Inc.

Connecticut General, through the holding company device, has in addition to three mutual funds, rapidly growing interests in land and real estate development.

The Insurance Company of North America, through its INA Corporation has acquired the well-known Blyth & Company, an investment company.

Other companies, many of them, have diversified in more or less similar fashion. Some have acquired credit card companies and computer outfits. U.S. Senator Philip A. Hart, chairman of the Senate Antitrust Subcommittee said, on March 27, 1969, "Most of the larger acquisitions involving insurers suggest violations of the antitrust laws." [37]

This picture, clear though it is, is extremely limited in range. What has taken place is almost incredible in scope.[38] Yet, it is not my purpose to point the finger at any individual stock life insurance company, or any group of them. The culprit is the system—the ownership of life insurance companies by stockholders.

A CONTESTED MERGER

The biggest merger of all, approved on May 23, 1970, by Connecticut Insurance Commissioner Cotter, and certain to be appealed, involves the acquisition by International Telephone and Telegraph Corporation of the Hartford Fire Insurance Company. The combined assets of the two companies, over $7 billion, make it the

---

[37] Critics of conglomerates, including Senator Hart, are more worried that the conglomerates may really have some inherent disadvantages as business operations. Some conglomerates, he fears, "may be jerry-built structures, sustained by various forms of financial and stock manipulation and the high growth rate resulting from frenetic merger activity." (Special Report On Conglomerates, published by *Business Week,* November 30, 1968).

[38] "At its best, the conglomerate style harkens back to the entrepreneurial spirit and daring that typified the early days of U.S. capitalism." (Ibid.)

largest corporate merger in United States history, exceeding the amalgamation that resulted in the Penn Central Company.

Many aspects make it appropriate in this study of stock insurance company financial manipulations. The fact that the Hartford Life Insurance Company was included makes it particularly relevant.[39] The proposal was under attack from the beginning. The Justice Department sought a preliminary injunction in October of 1969. It was denied by a Federal District Court in New Haven. It may ultimately reach the United States Supreme Court.

After approval by Connecticut Commissioner Cotter, who imposed restrictions on the transfer of funds by the fire insurance company to ITT, and other limitations, Ralph Nader, together with a Hartford Fire policyholder, announced their intention of blocking the merger. They charged that Mr. Cotter "failed to consider possible anti-competitive effects of the merger." They charged further that ITT would be free to remove the assets and surplus of Hartford Fire in the future for its own purposes, including corporate acquisitions and the financing of ITT operations and expansion plans. Mr. Nader seeks a ruling that Delaware holding companies (ITT was originally incorporated in Maryland and reincorporated in Delaware) should not be permitted to "take over" Connecticut insurance companies. "The new provisions of the Delaware law," Mr. Nader charges, "when applied to the control of an insurance company, are incompatible with the best interests of stockholders, policyholders and the public."

About two weeks prior to Mr. Cotter's approval of the merger, he received a letter of protest from Herbert S. Denenberg, professor of insurance in the Wharton School of the University of Pennsylvania. Since Professor Denenberg's observations were mostly confined to the effects of the merger on insurance operations, they deserve our attention. Among others, he made these points:

If this merger is consummated, ITT-Hartford will be in a position

---

[39] Of the 250,000 shares of outstanding stock of Hartford Life, the Hartford Fire Insurance Company owned 248,687.

to practice reciprocity on a grand scale without precedent in the insurance business. Reciprocity (which has been defined as the "use of one's purchasing power to obtain sales and the practice of preferring one's customers in purchasing"; in other words, it is: "You buy from me and I'll buy from you") has serious adverse effects on a competitive economy:

> Reciprocity permits a firm to increase sales without resorting to price competition; this kind of growth is often at the expense of its smaller competitors;

> Reciprocity permits intercorporate ties and connections to become more decisive than efficiency or price.

Thus reciprocity is an ideal technique for giant corporations to stifle competition, to destroy small competitors, and to undermine free enterprise.

ITT already has the massive purchasing power, in the range of $4 billion dollars, and the massive connections and controls, for effective utilization of reciprocity. By adding Hartford Insurance Company to its corporate family, it will have another ideal instrument for the practice of reciprocity. Hartford is the fourth largest property and liability insurance company in the United States and has an important market position in every major line of insurance in virtually every major market area. Insurance is ideal for the practice of reciprocity for a number of reasons. Every insurance transaction is not a logical candidate for reciprocity, of course, but there are a variety of factors that make insurance reciprocity-prone.

A company that is to take advantage of reciprocity needs a product to sell that their suppliers need. Insurance is ideal because everyone needs insurance. It is a universal economic necessity for every kind and size of business. Every business must buy a substantial amount of insurance. Every business is a substantial customer for insurance. This includes all kinds of property and liability insurance—fire insurance, automobile insurance, workmen's compensation insurance. In addition, businesses buy group life and health insurance for their employees.

An insurance company only doing an insurance business, unlike an industrial company, has little purchasing power for use in reciprocity. It simply doesn't buy very much. In 1969, property and liability insurers had premium and investment income of over $25 billion, but made purchases from other firms of somewhat over $1 billion.

Life insurers had $28 billion in premium income and made purchases from other firms somewhat in excess of $2 billion. So an insurance company by itself can barely scratch the surface of reciprocity opened up to an insurance company merged with an industrial giant. ITT-Hartford will have more purchasing power than the rest of the insurance industry put together.

The advent of the conglomerate and the holding company with insurance subsidiaries, like ITT, has opened up new vistas for the use of insurance in reciprocity arrangements. For the conglomerate or holding company now has insurance, the universal necessity, to sell; and it has purchasing power to favor those who buy insurance from it. Thus, the conglomerate or holding company will be in a position to get the insurance business it wants, massively across the board, or on a selective basis of "creaming." As one article on reciprocity has noted, "suppliers may be chosen for their desirability as customers and their susceptibility to reciprocity."

The ITT-Hartford merger would, therefore, contribute a substantial anti-competitive threat, while making another significant contribution to growing economic concentration that has dangerous potential for a free society and a free economy.

SANITY REARS ITS HEAD

Over a year before Professor Denenberg's warning, others saw danger in the successful take-over bids by conglomerates that had only a fraction of the assets of the insurance companies they hoped to swallow. Back in February 1969, James K. Kemper, Jr., president of Kemperco, Inc., said:

> I belong to the ranks of the skeptics. I believe that when the returns are all in, the record for public service, sound growth and profit of professional insurance organizations, managed by insurance people, will surpass that of all but a very few of the conglomerates which have invaded our business. It will surpass not only

59

their record in the insurance business, but their record for intelligent and profitable diversification.

When this becomes apparent—when the bloom is off the conglomerate rose—we might even see some victors become victims.[40]

Mr. Kemper, at that time, did not have a foreknowledge of the subsequent stock market collapse. "The conglomerates' security prices . . . are currently hovering at levels that are down 50% to 90% from their 1967–68 highs. . . . The fact is, however, that the sagging securities price of many conglomerates have placed them in a very vulnerable position and some of these former 'victors' might very well become takeover victims themselves." [41]

"No creation of the U.S. economy reflects the vigor, imagination, and sheer brass of the 1960s more than the conglomerate corporations. Wheeling and dealing with panache and merging with seeming haste all over the lot, they have shattered the cautious business clichés that have prevailed since the Depression. In so doing, they have mushroomed suddenly into some of the nation's largest industrial empires. Now they are in trouble." [42]

Charles J. Zimmerman, chairman of Connecticut Mutual Life, and one of the most respected of all life insurance executives, said, at the 1970 International Insurance Seminar in Tokyo, "The implications and consequences [of diversification at the corporate level] are not confined to any individual company, but affect the entire insurance business, and, beyond that, the entire economy. . . . Will diversification of service mergers and growth of holding companies result in unhealthy concentration of economic power, conflicts of interest, the threat of monopoly? These are the perfectly proper and necessary questions being asked. And these questions must be answered in the public interest." [43]

---

[40] Meeting of the New York Chapter of the Society CPCU.

[41] *The National Underwriter,* May 30, 1970.

[42] Special Report on Conglomerates, published by *Business Week,* November 30, 1968. Since then the "trouble" has sharpened materially.

[43] *The National Underwriter,* August 15, 1970.

I believe Mr. Zimmerman's questions were rhetorical. His conclusions seem obvious. When an executive of his stature sees the dangers he so well expressed, even the most rabid of the expansionists must experience some doubt about the directions he has taken.

The whole sad and dangerous performance, initiated and continued solely by stock companies in their race for profits, was summed up by Professor Herbert S. Denenberg in the April 1970 issue of the *Insurance Law Journal:*

> Anyone who reads the headlines has some knowledge of the rise of conglomerates, their interests in insurance companies, and the holding company, merger and diversification movement sweeping the industry.
>
> Here in Philadelphia there was the acquisition of Reliance Insurance Company by Leasco Data and rumors of attempted takeover of INA by Bangor Punta Corporation, a conglomerate; by AMK Corporation, a New York company; and by Levin-Townsend Computer Corporation.
>
> Conglomerate activities have reached the point where there is growing public alarm over the development.
>
> It adds up to a threat to insurance markets. To what extent will the whole conduct of the insurance business become secondary to market manipulations, intercorporate acquisitions, investment ploys, and the rest of the money game? Insurance has already been neglected due to overemphasis on investment.

These "diversifications," perhaps just as appealing to some mutual company managements, were not available to them. "A holding company cannot own a mutual, the policyholders do. So the holding company route has been denied to mutuals." [44] But some of the mutuals, driven competitively by the corporate metamorphoses of the stock companies, responded in the limited fashion permitted by state laws. They formed what came to be known as "downstream" holding companies, a means by which the mutuals could form and finance corporations that would in turn acquire and manage other

---

[44] "Dimensions of American Business," *Forbes,* May 15, 1969.

61

stock corporations.[45] But this device, fortunately, has strong brakes. The regulatory authorities must, and do, view the surpluses of the mutuals as the property of the policyholders, who are not deemed to be risk takers. The limitations of the "downstream" holding companies have been described by Laughlin and Kedzie in *Best's Review,* April 1970. In regard to the all-important availability-of-capital question, they pointed out:

> Since the DSHC is, in effect, a subsidiary of the mutual insurer, it cannot claim the earning power of the mutual insurance operations as is possible with a holding company set atop a stock insurer, where the insurer becomes the subsidiary of the holding company. It would seem to follow from this that one consequence is that the amount of debt financing available to the DSHC would be more limited than that available to the "upstream" type just described.
>
> We have seen an interesting situation develop with a newly formed USHC [Upstream holding company, the device of the stock companies] which, while showing insignificant amounts of assets, was pleasantly surprised by its ability to borrow relatively large amounts of capital as a result of the underlying asset strength of its insurance companies. Given the same size and type of companies, we cannot imagine that such capital would be available in anywhere near the same amounts if a DSHC were involved.

The significant point, however, is not whether upstream or downstream is more flexible or profitable. The point is that neither would have come into being without the inherent possibility of abuse in the stock ownership structure. Funds created overwhelmingly by policyholders, and only to a minor degree by stockholders, are used for the benefit of the latter, without the consent of the former and with the built-in possibility of loss to them.

This, then, is the immediate red light flashed by the stock life insurance structure.

---

[45] Union Mutual of Maine owns a downstream holding company, Union Mutual Corporation, which formed or acquired: Community Life Insurance Company, Union Equity Corporation, Claims Service International, and Financial Force Development Corporation.

A PRECEDENT FOR WHAT?

The most popular justification of diversification shenanigans, endlessly repeated by some life insurance officials, is the apocryphal explanation of the tragic decline of our railroads. It runs this way: the railroad officials had the naive belief that they were in the business of moving people and goods, in cars on tracks, when they should have realized that they were in the transportation business; that is to say that they should have known that their business included anything directly or remotely related to moving people and goods. This, of course, would have included airplanes, buses, automobiles, motorcycles, bicycles, and even hotels, travel agencies, and the development of new industrial and residential areas. (This curious view suggests also that the manufacturer of handkerchiefs is not merely in the business of supplying materials to aid people in politely relieving congested nasal passages, but is actually in the "nose" business, and thus should supply medicines, cosmetics, sunburn lotion, and related products. Extensions of such nonsense are both easy and unrewarding.)

In truth, however, the downward slide of the railroads was not traceable to a narrow view of functions, but rather to the very diversifications that some life insurance executives are obsessively trying to justify. *The Washington Post* of July 5, 1970, reported, "It may well be, as some congressmen suspect, that the [Penn Central] and other railroads, by the drive of railroad holding companies for diversification, have been drained of assets and profits that should have been put back into the business."

The New York Times of November 2, 1970, supported this observation with considerable evidence. It reported:

The diversification program was pursued by the Pennsylvania Railroad before it merged with the New York Central on February 1, 1968, to form the Penn Central.

The seven-page staff report [to the House Banking and Currency Committee] tells how, between 1963 and the end of 1965, the railroad made four major acquisitions through its wholly owned investment subsidiary, the Pennsylvania Company. These acquisitions were the Buckeye Pipe Line Company, the Great Southwest Corporation, the Arvida Corporation and the Macco Corporation. Buckeye is a crude oil and petroleum products pipeline concern; the other three companies are engaged in real estate investment and development. The four purchases, according to the staff report, involved payment of $144-million in cash, of which the Pennsylvania Company put up all but about $738,000. This balance was advanced directly by the railroad.

The staff report observes, "It would appear that the railroad might have realized a greater rate of return by simply investing in improving the railroad, rather than venturing into real estate development." The report also suggests that the railroad might even have better used the $144-million to reduce its own debt.

Referring to the findings of the staff, Mr. Patman estimated that the acquisition "of the real estate and other subsidiaries had resulted in at least a $175-million drain" on the railroad's financial resources.

The headline on *The New York Times* article read: PENNSY'S DIVERSIFICATION CALLED FACTOR IN COLLAPSE.

Thus, the simpleminded explanation of the demise of the railroads not only fails to provide a justification for life insurance holding company diversification, but is actually a potent argument against it.

THE STRANGE WAYS OF CONGLOMERATES

It is commonly believed that our country has come a long way from the old days of unrestrained capitalist expansion. The robber barons of the nineteenth century, we now think, are nothing more than a bad memory. The emergence of the conglomerates, however, demands a rethink. *Business Week,* you may recall, said, "At its best, the conglomerate style harkens back to the entrepreneurial

spirit and daring that typified the early days of U.S. capitalism."
In support of that observation, its Special Report On Conglomerates pointed out that in order "to get leverage, a conglomerate will go through some of the most complicated financial contortions."

The contortions include tax loss carry-overs, tricky accounting procedures, and sometimes the criminal use of other people's money. An examination of the new style is both distressing and rewarding.

WHEN IS A BAD DEAL ADVANTAGEOUS?

Donald Kramer, an insurance stock specialist, and a partner in the New York firm, Oppenheimer & Company, shed a good deal of light on the acquisition of noninsurance businesses by insurance companies in an interview with the *National Underwriter,* reported by that publication on September 12 and September 19, 1970. He explained why "the competition for bad deals . . . is intense," by stating that among the deals

> are a large insurer and stock brokerage house. This particular insurer has a huge tax loss carry-forward. It could use every tax deductible dollar it could find, so it buys the brokerage house for some $55 million and the brokerage house promptly loses money. Another large insurer has a tax loss carry-forward that rivals General Dynamics' greatest moments so it buys a large computer firm for $75 million and incurs a huge loss for tax purposes.

> The competition for bad deals in this industry is intense. Take the case of a large property insurer who, in a period of enormously high interest rates, sterilizes some $100 million in an investment in a low yielding life company—and then offers to acquire it on terms that would result in a 30 cent per share dilution. Subsequently, it acquires an interest in a credit card company and manages to take a $13 million write-off which gives the credit card firm a tax loss carry-forward for 10 years.

ARCANE, CRYPTIC, ENIGMATIC

Abraham J. Briloff, professor of accountancy in the Baruch College of the City University of New York, spelled out some questionable accounting procedures, in the *Notre Dame Lawyer,* issue of Summer 1970. Under the caption "Conglomerates and Insurance Companies—a Symbiotic Relationship," Professor Briloff wrote:

> Having thus described the several alternatives for business combinations, those of "dirty pooling," "polluted purchase," and for want of a better descriptive term, the hybrid "jackass," let me round out this phase of the discussion by summarizing the divergent practices pursued by three conglomerates in their accountings for their acquisitions of fire and casualty insurance companies. I will here describe the practices followed by Leasco Data Processing Equipment Corporation on its acquisition of the Reliance Insurance Company; by City Investing of Home Insurance; and by National General of Great American Insurance.
>
> It is more than coincidence that the conglomerates directed their acquisitive bent towards these insurance companies. The conglomerates coveted the insurers' huge pools of liquidity, their cash flow, and, as will be discerned presently, their latent pools of suppressed profits represented by the unrealized appreciation in their portfolios over the century or more of their respective security accumulations. There was, then, a symbiotic relationship formed between the conglomerates and insurance companies. Let us see how each of these three conglomerates has used or abused the accounting practices which have been alluded to.

His references to the acquisition of Great American Insurance by National General are sufficient for an understanding of the unusual accounting procedures that appear so prevalent. He wrote:

> The saga regarding the third of the conglomerate-insurance company tandems is still incomplete, since National General recently indicated a switch in its fiscal year reporting from September 30 to December 31. But yet there are anticipatory indications of income injection, using the insurance company portfolios as the catalyst.

In its fifty-two-week interim report (through last September 23) National General included as a part of its reported investment income, "net realized gains of $10,286,000." In view of the fact that this was the "Year of the Bear" this income amount is remarkable on two counts. First, in the January 10, 1969, prospectus renewing the exchange offer for Great American shares, National General assured us that: "For purposes of National financial statements, the Great American investments . . . initially will be valued at market, and net gains or losses realized by Great American which are attributable to increases or decreases in value prior to National's acquisition will not be included in National's reported income." Second, Great American has reported that it suffered an actual economic loss in its investment values of about $31 million during the nine months ended September 30, 1969.

Now how National General was able to pick up $10 million in gains when the insurance company statements reflect an actual major shrinkage for the period essentially coinciding with NG's control thereof is presently beyond my comprehension. The definitive 1969 statements expected to be promulgated over the next month or two might provide the answers. Is it possible that the assurances in their prospectuses notwithstanding, NG has been given the kind of head start the auditors gave to City Investing? Alternatively, has National pursued an eclectic policy whereby it disposed of securities that showed appreciation subsequent to the acquisition, all the while permitting losses to lie fallow and to fester?

One final note on this acquisition. After its takeover National General demonstrated that Leasco was a "Little Leaguer" when it took out but $39 million from Reliance. National raised the ante with an actual withdrawal of $174,540,824 as a dividend.

Again, at the very time when there is an urgent need for increases in our insurance underwriting potential we see illustrations of drains by but two conglomerates of more than $200 million of liquid insurance reserves. Add to this the shrinkage in reserves resulting from the substantial reductions in "admitted asset values" triggered by the precipitous declines in stock market prices and we can see why insurance has become very much of a "seller's market."

Clearly, then, there are critical deficiencies in our process of accountability whereby corporate managements are capable of managing and massaging their earnings by huge injections of specious income bundles—amounts of reported income not achieved by the managements claiming credit therefor, or amounts which are merely half-truths in that they reveal gains which have been nominally realized while ignoring completely the stagnant pools of losses.

Did strange accounting methods also feature the City Investing Company's acquisition of the Home Insurance Company? "In a single move, City's net worth went from $91 million to $610 million, while liabilities remained the same." [46]

"When a company is absorbed by a conglomerate, it generally disappears as a statistical entity, even though it may continue doing business with the same customers, at the same stand, under the same name. Its earnings are simply thrown into a common pool, and there is no way of telling whether its profits are higher or lower under the bigger corporate tent. Moreover, there is no effective way to gauge whether the tent itself is growing at a sustainable rate. Some conglomerates have made mergers to obscure a weak earnings record by divisions already in the company fold." [47]

The present SEC Act requires that conglomerates seeking to acquire an insurance company by a tender offer must disclose all information on the operations and the reasons for the tender offer when the acquisition exceeds 10 percent of the stock. SEC Chairman Hamer H. Budge, in favoring a bill that would extend disclosure rules to acquisitions of 5 percent, said, "There is evidence that companies undertaking an acquisition, limit their prior purchases of stock in the open market to around 9 percent as a means of avoiding making disclosures to the investing public."

A COMPANY IS BOUGHT WITH ITS OWN ASSETS

A most interesting case, illustrative of current machinations of stock-owned insurance companies (although a life company was

---

[46] *Business Week,* November 30, 1968.

[47] "Special Report on Conglomerates," *Business Week,* November 30, 1968.

only indirectly involved), was decided in the highest Appellate Court in New York State on July 1, 1970. If one wishes a course on how to buy an insurance company with its own assets, it is recommended that he read Judge Breitel's decision in People v. Sweeney and others, involving the Manhattan Casualty Company of New York. If discovered in time, the perpetrator will, of course, be convicted. The basic transaction of the case in point was so complicated that it was discovered too late. Judge Breitel said:

> These transactions, now time-barred, were simply a cover-up of a misappropriation of Manhattan's assets in January, 1962. The cover-up has been successful because, unfortunately, the indictment rests on a mistaken premise.

The State of New York was prosecuting an indictment which, as Judge Breitel of that Court stated in his opinion, "arose out of the purchase of the capital stock of Manhattan Casualty Company, a domestic insurer, paid for unlawfully with $5,000,000 of its own liquid assets."

However, the crimes charged in the indictment did not relate to this unlawful use of Manhattan's assets, but to the alleged concealment of the true transaction by manipulations with various bank certificates of deposit. The indictment alleged that these certificates of deposit were securities owned by Manhattan Casualty Company and had been pledged in violation of the Insurance Law. The defendants contended that a certificate of deposit is not a "security" and even if it were, the certificates were not Manhattan's property and that if they are treated as Manhattan's property, then Manhattan received the loan proceeds. These were the principal issues on the trial under discussion.

Judge Breitel's opinion recites that in 1962 Manhattan Casualty Company was purchased by one James F. Begole for $5 million from Bankers Life. By a complicated transaction involving a $5 million check from a bank, Begole received an envelope containing the shares of stock of Manhattan Casualty Company. Judge Breitel summed up the transaction with this language:

The effect of the transaction was that Manhattan's stock had been purchased with proceeds from the sale of Manhattan's government bonds. Begole now held Manhattan's stock. Bankers Life had been paid for the stock with the Irving Trust check, Irving Trust's check had been covered by the proceeds from the sale of the bonds, and Manhattan's bond box was empty of the government bonds. That emptiness, and the deviation from the corporate resolution to use the bonds to purchase a certificate of deposit, had now to be concealed. For that there was a prior plan for a camouflage transaction.

and later followed it with the statement:

This transaction was a complete wash or circular transaction, and its purpose was a camouflage.

As an end result, however, the Court of Appeals dismissed the indictment upon the ground that the certificates of deposit were never assets of Manhattan.

Surely, life insurance companies on which millions of Americans depend for the future security of their dependents, should not be permitted to operate in a climate exemplified by the curious things I have described.

THE SHOCKING PARADE OF NEW STOCK LIFE INSURANCE COMPANIES

Nothing in the entire history of American life insurance can match, in terms of speculative greed and potential dangers to policyholders, the incredible proliferation of new stock life insurance companies over the last quarter of a century. At the end of World War II there were 473 [48] life insurance companies operating in our country. By 1950, there were 611 [49] (exclusive, of course, of those new ones

---

[48] *Life Insurance Fact Book 1960.*

[49] Ibid.

that had suffered an early disappearance). In the following nineteen years, 2,229 [50] new companies were formed, all of them owned by stockholders,[51] and 1,060 retired, discontinued, or otherwise became nonexistent.

"Regulation for solvency is what we have known. When a company's assets were less than its liabilities, we threw it into the tank. Most of the life companies were sold off rather than liquidated, but to many the effect was the same." [52]

Exactly why those newly formed companies slipped into oblivion is impossible to determine. "Some firms disappear through mergers, consolidations, etc. Others are forced to quit by financial problems. It's difficult to single out all of the hardship cases because weak companies—or their outstanding policies—are often taken over by successful ones before they slip into insolvency." [53]

The rescue act, however, is not very dependable. "Purchase of existing companies . . . cannot become an industry-wide solution since there are many more life insurers than buy-out candidates." [54] And, of those "many more life insurers" a considerable number are in dire need of rescue. Responding to a question raised at the Chicago Conference on the Financial Congeneric, William D. Smith, of Millman and Robertson, a nationally known actuarial firm, said that of the 1,200 or so life companies that are in trouble, a number recognize and will resolve their problems, but the number that will do so cannot be readily determined.[55] In addition to all those re-

---

[50] *Life Insurance Fact Book 1969,* and *Best's Review,* March 1970.

[51] The experiences of two states, New York with the most effective insurance regulation, and Arizona with perhaps the weakest, vividly illustrate the extent of the new stock company explosion. In the twenty-year period following midcentury, thirty-seven new stock life insurance companies were formed in New York State. During the first *fifty* years of the century only eight stock companies were incorporated there. Arizona had three companies in 1950, and three hundred and thirty-three in mid-1969. Moreover the final figure does not include the substantial number that disappeared during the twenty-year period.

[52] Illinois Insurance Director James Baylor, at the 1970 annual seminar for Life executives, at Chicago, quoted by *The National Underwriter,* October 3, 1970.

[53] *Changing Times, The Kiplinger Magazine,* May 1965.

[54] "The Management Of Innovation," J. Finley Lee, *CLU Journal,* April 1970.

[55] *The National Underwriter,* October 11, 1969.

insured, merged, taken over, and put out of business by state authorities during the last ten years, a minimum of 126 companies just disappeared through retirement, dissolution, liquidation, or withdrawal.[56]

Quite obviously, the final returns on the explosive new company proliferation are not yet in. The raison d'être of the new formations, however, is perfectly clear. *Changing Times, The Kiplinger Magazine* warned its readers, in May 1965: "Watch out for stock promoters who are less interested in building up a strong company than in making a fast buck profit. The Securities and Exchange Commission has already taken action against several. In one case, company insiders were charged with selling stock at $10 a share that they had bought on options for $2. The $10 buyers were not told that the money was going into the insiders' pockets instead of the company's treasury."

Melvin L. Gold, consulting actuary, at the Conference on the Financial Congeneric, according to *The National Underwriter* of October 11, 1969, said that the managements of many small life companies have forsaken this objective [operational earnings] in favor of corporate adventures and misadventures. "When you can't cope with internal problems," he was reported to have said, "distract your stockholders—form a holding company."

The SEC had made a staff study of the sharp rise in the filing of registration statements by new companies for public offerings of stock. Their study showed that 70 percent of the life companies so filing had five years or less of experience. The staff report expressed alarm:

> It is obvious from a cursory review of the Commission's News Digest over the past few months that the public is being deluged with a torrent of securities offerings by life insurance companies. Many of these offerings involved unusual distribution methods not normally encountered in the sale of securities of nonlife insurance issuers. Also, many of these offerings are being made by companies

---

[56] *Best's Life News,* March 1961 through March 1967.
Best's Insurance News, March 1968.
Best's Review, March 1967 and March 1970.

that do not have any history of operation or do not have a history of profitable operations. In some cases, the market price for the securities of these companies has been manipulated or the securities have been sold by fraud.

WHO PUSHED THE STOCK?

Brokers specializing in new life insurance company stock were having a field day with gullible, profit-hungry investors. Levering Cartwright, President of Cartwright, Valleau and Company of Chicago, and an outstanding authority on life insurance stock, with the additional attribute of understanding the structure and operations of life insurance companies, wrote in late 1960:

"The motives range from a radiant conviction to the meanest spirit of stock jobbing. From a genuine desire to participate in and promote the finest traditions of life insurance, to exploitation of the wonderful reputation of the business for hit and run gains of 15% commissions on stock sales and stock option schemes. A medley of innocence and contrivance, with here and there, let it be fairly said, hard-headed purposeful and knowledgeable undertakings." [57]

Four years later Mr. Cartwright used sharper language. He said then:

"The type of salesman selling stocks in the new companies is fully aware of what it takes to move these stocks. They are the kind that come out of the woodwork, and when things cool off, they go back into the woodwork. Since 1957, insurance stocks have been a big thing. It is pitiful to see what the public is biting on this year. This kind of thing, going on all over the country, is dynamite."

He referred to the new company situation as reaching scandalous proportions, and added:

"Although there are a lot of well intentioned people involved, it is a pretty cynical operation these days." [58]

---

[57] *The National Underwriter,* November 5, 1960.

[58] *The National Underwriter,* November 14, 1964.

TO MAKE A BUCK

Obviously, before the salesmen and the buyers of the stock got into the act, the promoters of the new companies had to ring up the curtain. What were their motives?

> We have frequently had occasion to ask the managements of these new companies as to their motivation for entering the life insurance business. After all, are not the hundreds of existing carriers quite capable of servicing the public needs? The answer to our query was, in the last analysis, nearly always, "Why, of course, to make money for ourselves. . . ."
>
> The quest for personal gain is entirely valid and praiseworthy in a capitalist economy, but there exists, as we see it, certain hidden weaknesses in the frank admission by a great many new entrants to this business, that they have neither the capacity nor the intention of adding anything really new to the state of the art. After all, young companies in other fields usually offer some rationale for existing beyond merely earning a profit. They fulfill a need of some sort. The small electronics firm quite frequently has inventive ideas which may represent an improvement upon existing techniques. The new retailer, to succeed, must ordinarily have lower prices, superior location, or both.[59]

In elaborating on this issue of new company proliferation, my point is not that stock life insurance company management is essentially wicked, or that all new company formations were motivated by greed, or even that all brokers specializing in life insurance stocks misled their customers. My point is simply that the stock company structure invites corruption of the life insurance process— a process so essential to the aspirations of the American people that corruption cannot be tolerated.

The management of life insurance demands a deep appreciation

---

[59] "The Hazards and Rewards of Investing In Small Life Insurance Companies," a report by Equity Research Associates, prepared for Filor, Bullard & Smyth, October 15, 1964.

of the public interest, a recognition of its fiduciary nature, and a keen sense of trusteeship. The promoters and managers of many of the new companies either had no awareness of their responsibilities, or deliberately disregarded them. "The trouble is that many newly formed companies seem . . . to put the publics in precisely the reverse order—stockholders first, field underwriters and home office employees second, and policyholders last." [60]

DARK CLOUDS WERE SEEN

Although precious little was actually done about these new company formations, a number of state insurance commissioners expressed strong opposition. William E. Timmons, Iowa Commissioner, and former president of the National Association of Insurance Commissioners said:

> The brief history and way of life of many of the newly-formed companies demonstrates dramatically that their organizers and management men do not have the mettle, the courage, or the ability to do things right. It is important for all of us to realize that a life insurance company is no place to experiment with management capability or the integrity of men. We need to create a climate where the fast buck artist and the Mickey Mouse policy cannot exist. I have an uneasy feeling that termites are right now actively at work on the foundations of the life insurance industry.[61]

California Commissioner, Stafford Grady, said, ". . . it is not proper that new insurers be organized for the purpose of enabling promoters to profit in the transaction of the stock of the corporation." [62] Henry Root Stern, Jr., New York Superintendent, expressed his deep concern in these words:

---

[60] William H. Schmidt, Senior Vice-President, Mutual Life of New York, at the 1966 Conference of Actuaries in Public Practice.

[61] Annual American Life Convention Meeting, Toronto, as reported by *The National Underwriter*, October 23, 1965.

[62] *The National Underwriter*, January 9, 1965.

It has been further argued that such risk-taking is not a matter of Insurance Department concern. I do not agree with these arguments, if for no other reason than the unfortunate effect which speculation in new life company stocks can have upon the image of the entire insurance industry and that of State Regulation.

These two soft spots under the foundations of a recently-formed life insurer—the long and uncertain wait for returns on investment, and the speculative inflation of its stock values—are a matter of concern between the company's management and its investors. Since these problems may not directly involve the company's services to policyholders, some observers might think that they would be of little concern to the Insurance Department. Nothing could be further from the truth because the sad day may come when disillusioned impatience on the part of the investors, accompanied by a decline in the speculative popularity of the company's stock, may coincide with urgent and quite predictable need for additional capitalization. At that point policyholder interest would be immediately affected by the company's financial straits. This foreseeable peril is clearly a Department concern.[63]

The efforts of some diligent state insurance departments succeeded in slowing down the parade of new companies, but it hasn't yet been stopped. Indeed, it is still quite a spectacle. In 1969, when fifty-four companies "retired," eighty-nine new ones joined the march. But back in 1965, births exceeded deaths by a hundred and six!

SOME JUICY FAILURES

The mortality rate of new life companies can be spelled out statistically, but the causes of death have not been determined. Some, of course, were "acquired," but others just folded. There is no way, as yet, to determine exactly what happened to those 1,060 "disappearances," between 1950 and 1969. There have been charges of criminal violations and of underworld influence and control. According to *Newsday*, July 10, 1970, "Last year, insurance compa-

---

[63] New York City Underwriters Association Sales Congress, March 11, 1965.

nies in Arizona, Oklahoma and Florida were declared insolvent because of complex swindles involving known underworld figures."

The National Underwriter of September 17, 1970, quoted Aaron M. Kohn, managing director of the Metropolitan Crime Commission of New Orleans, as follows:

> A Louisiana-based financier includes among his many controlled corporations ownership of a life insurance business in various states. He also controls a bank in which the Cosa Nostra boss's son serves on the board of directors. He has ownership interests in at least four other life insurance companies. His financial involvements with two state supreme court justices brought about the resignation of one after a Federal tax prosecution. Recently, through a known front, he has acquired a Delaware corporation headquartered in Atlanta, now seeking to take over an insolvent insurer with home office in Salt Lake City.
>
> Insurance company funds have helped capitalize Las Vegas gambling casinos.
>
> Last month, at the American Bar Association convention in St. Louis, Ralph Salerna reported that the biggest numbers-gambling racketeer in Indianapolis bought out an entire insurance company, lock, stock and barrel.
>
> Sometime ago I learned about negotiations of a national life insurance company with two labor union bosses for group insurance, with indirect kickback inducements. Both labor bosses, according to our information, have a history of economic alliance with La Cosa Nostra's boss in Louisiana, Carlos Marcello.

According to *The National Underwriter,* "[Mr. Kohn] explained to the press exactly why organized crime would seek to move into insurance. Basically, he said, it needs such corporate entities as insurance companies, loan companies, and savings and loan associations to, first, hide its illegally acquired capital and then to use the investment medium as a means of moving that capital into still other investments either legal or illegal. A favorite route is outright acquisition as opposed to just minority stock investment, because it permits criminal organizations to own and control the records of the business and the movement of their capital."

New York State's outstanding insurance department found the young Hamilton Life insolvent in 1968, took possession of its property and undertook rehabilitation pursuant to court order.[64] It appears that policyholders will suffer no losses whatever. Not nearly so fortunate, however, are the policyholders of the National Capitol Life of Alabama, formed in early 1966. After some three years of operations it was placed in receivership by an Alabama Circuit Court and enjoined from writing new insurance "because of fraudulent disposition of assets by some of the officers and directors." Accordingly, the receiver informed the insureds that "payment of cash surrender value . . . or any other claims under your contract, will be made, based on funds available, subject to order of the court. It will take some time to determine the assets available and the fractional sums due. . . . At this writing it is clear that full payment . . . will not be possible." [65]

Illustrative of hanky-panky is the plight of National Producers Life Insurance Company of Phoenix, Arizona, placed in receivership by an order of the Superior Court of Maricopa County on December 8, 1969. According to *Insuranceflash* of May 12, 1970, Arizona Director of Insurance Millard Humphrey charged that National Producers Life was defrauded of some $24 million. Defendants in the Federal Court proceeding include Alabama National Life and Old National Life Insurance Company, both of Montgomery, Alabama, and National Securities, Inc., of Phoenix, as well as six individuals.

Insuranceflash reported that the complaint recited that on August 1, 1967, National Securities secured control of National Producers. Two of the individual defendants owned controlling interests in National Securities, and another defendant owned controlling

---

[64] Hamilton Life's chairman, Philip J. Goldberg, later became chairman of the now defunct Financial Security Life of Arizona. Late in 1970, he was indicted by a Federal grand jury, along with four others, on charges of using worthless annuity policies as collateral for loans of more than a million dollars. (*The National Underwriter,* November 24, 1970).

[65] Photostatic copy of letter to policyholders sent to the author by the receiver on February 9, 1970.

interests in the two Alabama companies, in addition to being an officer of National Securities. In what was a complicated agreement, the Alabama firms presumably obtained over 1.2 million shares of National Producers, in exchange for mortgages, stock in other firms, and real estate, of less value. Apparently the deficiency was $24 million.

As of September 22, 1970, National Producers Life was still in receivership. According to the Arizona Department of Insurance this action was taken for the purpose of "conserving the assets of the company for the benefit of the policyholders and stockholders."

Both Alabama National Life and Old National were placed in receivership on March 28, 1970, by the Circuit Court of Jefferson County, Alabama. Thus all three life insurance companies involved in the National Producers Life situation are in the hands of receivers.

(The business of Alabama National was transferred to American Benefit Life of New Orleans on March 31, 1970.)

In another juicy action [66] Jimmie J. Ryan, president of the Community Life Insurance Company of Tulsa, Oklahoma, pleaded guilty on June 8, 1970, to a conspiracy count that alleged scheming to get unlawful loans from banks in seven states. He also admitted unlawful scheming in specific letters to the Chase Manhattan Bank on three occasions during 1968. Mr. Ryan explained in the United States District Court that he engaged in what he knew to be "an unlawful criminal agreement" with three other individuals because "I thought at the time that it would be beneficial to Community National." One of his codefendants was described by a defense lawyer as "a very undesirable and greasy character with a long record as a con man."

Mr. Ryan admitted one count of conspiracy, including false statements and omissions of data in deals by other defendants to obtain bank loans amounting to about $700,000 using life insurance policies as collateral. The insurance policies allegedly were traded by Community National for about 700,000 shares of stock of Tintair,

---

[66] *The New York Times,* May 9, 1970.

Inc. The participants were accused of failing to tell banks that made loans against the policies, of a secret agreement that limited the value of the insurance.

Federal officials said that Community National Life was put in the hands of a receiver in July 1969. According to his report, Community National had $8.4 million of admitted assets at the end of 1969; its liabilities at the time amounted to $17.9 million.[67] In addition to the Oklahoma action, the operations of Community National Life were suspended in Arkansas and Florida. As recently as October 1970, a major stockholder of Community National Life filed a $52 million suit against officers and directors of the company, alleging that they wasted and mismanaged assets resulting in "a state of insolvency."[68]

Another situation tends to make clear the not uncommon financial shenanigans indulged in by some stock life insurance companies. The United Founders Life of Oklahoma City was directed by the Missouri Insurance Superintendent, in May 1970, to cease writing new business in Missouri, pending completion of a departmental examination then in progress.

The Missouri department said that the action was taken as a result of "discrepancies in several areas concerning the operations of United Founders Life and after a directive was issued to the company by the Oklahoma Commissioner requesting additional deposits for the protection of Oklahoma policyholders."

---

[67] The receiver, Mr. Rolle, concedes he hasn't decided what to do about one "asset" he discovered after taking charge of the insurer: a plush suite of hidden rooms and secret passages in the company's headquarters, since dubbed "The Lair."

The private sanctuary was discovered as Mr. Rolle tried to track down a telephone listed as belonging to the company but not to be found in the office areas. An automatic elevator offered the first clue: it had a button for floor one, then a keyhole, then a button for floor two. The keyhole, it turned out, represented a mezzanine. On this floor was a smoked glass mirror covering an entire wall and concealing a door. Behind the door was the lavish "Lair," complete with a wine "cellar" and marble-topped bar with tap beer from a refrigerator in the basement. One gaudily decorated room included a color television and stereophonic record player. A bedroom, with a fur-covered king-sized bed, was to one side. Off that was a black-carpeted, gold-walled dressing room and a bath with ruby red lavatories, gold fixtures, and a double shower. (*Wall Street Journal,* June 8, 1970)

[68] *The National Underwriter,* October 14, 1970.

A regularly scheduled examination for solvency was being conducted by several states, according to the Missouri department. In December 1969, a hearing on the merger of Modern Security Life of Springfield, Missouri, with United Founders resulted in disapproval of the merger by a three-man commission board, with the Missouri Commissioner as Chairman.[69]

At the present writing, a paradoxical situation exists. On September 22, 1970, I was informed by the Missouri Division of Insurance, that while "during the year 1969, there were 2 complaints filed in [our] office against the company, it is currently authorized to conduct its business in the State of Missouri." However, United Founders Life was served with a restraining order on September 18, 1970, "granted by the district court of Oklahoma county that prohibited it from engaging in the insurance business until a hearing on October 2, [1970]. The order was granted on application of Oklahoma Commissioner Joe B. Hunt, who alleged that the insurer is insolvent." [70] However, the Oklahoma district court judge modified the September eighteenth order, thus permitting the insurer to resume operations at least temporarily. The judge ordered an accounting firm to provide him with an independent certified balance sheet showing the financial condition of the insurer as of September thirtieth, no later than November thirtieth. The Court set an appointment for a full hearing on the latter date.[71]

The story of Federated Security Life Insurance Company of Utah is complex indeed, and illustrative of intricate financial moves, not uncommon among newer stock companies. According to *Insuranceflash* of May 18, 1970, the Utah Insurance Commissioner, in his order to show cause, dated October 6, 1969, stated that his department started an examination of Federated Security in February of that year and discovered the company's assets short by some $6 million. An examiner of the Utah Department was appointed manager for the company in a rehabilitation proceeding after the Utah Third Judicial Court had granted a rehabilitation order. The Utah

---

[69] *The National Underwriter,* June 6, 1970.

[70] *The National Underwriter,* September 26, 1970.

[71] *The National Underwriter,* October 3, 1970.

Commissioner then filed suit in U.S. District Court in Salt Lake City against the individuals and organizations that presumably had bought Federated Security Life. The complaint alleged fraud, conversion, and breach of judiciary duties by the defendants and demanded the return of over $6 million allegedly removed from the assets of the company.

Insuranceflash, in presenting in detailed fashion the various maneuvers that resulted in the $6 million shortage, asked, "Did the present 'owners' of Federated Security buy the company with its own assets?" The pending action, according to *Insuranceflash,* "alleged that when the Insurance Department asked how come somebody departed with Federated Security's $6 million, it was told that Peoples Bond and Mortgage Company had 'replaced' these securities with mortgages of equal value, but states that these mortgages really didn't belong to Federated Security because F. S. executives had later executed re-assignments of the mortgages to Peoples Bond & Mortgage. . . . On January 14, 1970, U.S. District Judge . . . at Salt Lake . . . issued an injunction restraining Peoples Bond and Mortgage from selling the $6 million of mortgages, and also issued another injunction against three companies [involved in the Federated Security transaction] restraining the sale, transfer or other disposition of the Transwestern Life [of Montana], also involved shares . . ."

Previously, on November 19, 1969, the Superior Court of the State of California, on application of the Insurance Commissioner of that state, ordered that he "is hereby appointed Conservator in California of Federated Security Insurance Company, a Utah corporation . . . and directed as such Conservator to conduct the business of [that company]." The Court's decision was based on the fact that Federated Security "is in such condition that it is insolvent within the meaning of the Insurance Code and that its further transaction of business will be hazardous to its policyholders, its creditors, and to the public."

In response to a letter of mine, C. N. Ottosen, Utah Commissioner of Insurance, wrote on October 30, 1970, "Due to a very unfortunate incident, a large block of the assets of [Federated

Security Life] were removed from the Company by a trusted officer and as yet have not been returned. The company was thrown into rehabilitation proceedings on November 5, 1969, and lawsuits were started in the court to recover those moneys. At the present time the Federal Court lawsuits are still pending, but about four companies have submitted rehabilitation programs to the local court. . . . Therefore, in direct answer to your letter, the company has not been selling insurance but the business has been retained and its present operator is merely keeping the company in business until one of these other programs can be selected and the company brought back on its feet to the point where it can enter into the regular business of an insurance company."

This brief review of the Federated Security Life situation omits many of the lurid details as well as the names of the many individuals and corporations who participated. The actions of the Insurance Commissioners and the Courts, however, give the flavor of the various dealings that took place.

Nevada State Commissioner, Louis J. Mastos, told the 1970 National Association of Life Companies annual meeting that in his five years in office he had to put into receivership three of the state's five domiciled life insurance companies. The main problem, he explained, involved reshuffling of assets, inflating of asset values, and commissions on stock between principals.[72]

LEGISLATORS TOO?

Quite obviously, it is impossible for a legislator to have a financial interest in a mutual life insurance company. Equally obviously, it is possible for him to own stock, or possess stock options, in a stock company. And many legislators do, notwithstanding the obvious conflict of interest. Sometimes the stock is purchased at market prices. More often it is purchased for less, and not infre-

---

[72] *The National Underwriter*, August 8, 1970.

quently stock options are made available—particularly by new companies.

Dr. Willis P. Rokes, chairman of the department of insurance at the University of Nebraska, recently referred to this type of abuse. He said, "The large number of insurer bankruptcies and liquidations occurring in recent years, resulting in losses of millions of dollars to the public, has focused attention on the quality of state regulation. In Florida, for example, a survey by the *Miami Herald* revealed an unusual potential for conflict of interest, since one-half of Florida legislators in 1969 had insurance interests or had a pecuniary involvement with the industry. Florida legislators were found to have been closely connected with several insurance companies that had slipped into bankruptcy or faced liquidation. These are the people who draft the laws regulating every facet of the insurance industry." [73]

Of course, all stock life insurance companies do not provide such financial incentives to legislators and regulators. But the conclusion that the stock company structure permits it is inescapable.

THE TRUTH ABOUT REINSURANCE

The partial or total loss of cash values by living policyholders may not be catastrophic, but what of the death claims by beneficiaries? In cases of insolvency, they will simply join the line of creditors, and receive perhaps ten cents on the dollar, if that.

The settlement of death claims suggests a frequently ignored or misunderstood aspect of the new company proliferation. Undercapitalized, the new company cannot afford the risk of a substantial early death claim. Thus its "retention" of a large new policy is limited to a minor portion of the face amount, and the balance "reinsured" in an established company that can accept the risk. Such larger policies are almost invariably sold by successful agents of the old-line companies (the new company being unable to house

---

[73] *The National Underwriter,* July 18, 1970.

an agent) who have been lured by the promise of stock options, directly related to their sales volume. The larger buyers, being reasonably sophisticated, frequently question the wisdom of placing the insurance with an unknown company. The agent, with an eye on his stock options, reassures his prospect by informing him that perhaps 90 percent of the coverage will be reinsured in a century-old company, with assets of hundreds of millions of dollars.

This aspect of reinsurance can be dramatically illustrated by an actual case. Early in 1965, the Trans World Life of New York, whose license may still have had wet ink, announced the sale of a $2,000,000 policy. Its retention at the time was only $15,000. (The fact that Trans World included the entire $2,000,000 as insurance in force is irrelevant to this issue.)

The amount reinsured in any situation in which a company issues a policy in excess of its own retention is actually a different kind of coverage for the policyholder. The amount retained by the original company will pass, by contract, directly to the beneficiary on the death of the insured. The amount reinsured will not so pass. "The liability of the reinsurer is to the ceding company and not to the policyholder on whose life the reinsurance is based. The funds paid by the reinsurer to the ceding company in settlement of a claim become a part of, and are merged with, the general funds of that company and are not segregated for the purpose of paying the specific claim to the beneficiary under the policy." [74]

Should the original company, at that time, be insolvent, the beneficiary will simply await liquidation results. The fact is that where reinsurance is involved, the strength of the reinsurance company is no greater than that of the original company.

No one has spelled this out in such unmistakable terms as has David G. Scott, President of Continental Assurance of Chicago. He said:

> The flaw in the argument of the agent who made the sale [in a new life company reinsuring the amount in excess of its retention] lies in his statement that because Continental Assurance Company

---

[74] *Life Insurance Trends at Mid-Century,* Walter O. Menge.

reinsures that small company—or this new company—that the credit back of the policy is just as good as if it were issued by Continental itself. I'd like to explain what would happen if a reinsured company managed to get into trouble at some future date and were to find itself in a position of insolvency.

If it does find itself in that position and it is not able to meet its obligations, then when the policy sold by it becomes a death claim, we would, of course, pay whatever amount we insured to the liquidator of the little company. But we wouldn't turn that money over to the insured. What he [the liquidator] would do is distribute that money, with the other assets of the company, pro-rata to all the creditors, so that the insured would only get his fair portion of the policy, just the same as any other creditor.

The fact that the policy was reinsured by Continental does not guarantee the payment of that death claim to a beneficiary in any way, shape or form. This means, of course, that if you have a policyholder who is thinking of purchasing a policy in one of these newer companies, you ought to be in a position to enlighten him that the same credit does not stand back of that new policy as stands back of one issued by Continental Assurance Company.[75]

The new company parade, then, had many people marching in its ranks. The promoters were joined by the original profit-hungry backers, by brokers specializing in life company stock, by greedy and gullible investors, and finally by agents, who faced with a conflict of interests, consciously or unconsciously misled their clients about the meaning of reinsurance. The real culprit, however, is not an individual or group. The culprit is the stock life insurance structure.

THE PENDULUM HAS SWUNG BACK

J. Owen Stalson, in his classic *Marketing Life Insurance*, described the aftermath of the 1905 Armstrong Investigation, in these words: "The speculative appeal gave way to the conservative, and

---

[75] A Continental Assurance Company Publication, "On The Level," October 30, 1964.

protection, not profits, became the theme of life insurance marketing." Mr. Stalson wrote that in 1940, after the mutualization of leading stock companies, and before the great proliferation of new ones began. I doubt that he would write it today.

More descriptive of the current scene were the observations of William O. Sahm, president of the Life Insurance Company of Illinois, made before A Conference For Young Life Insurance Companies in Chicago, September 1 and 2, 1965. He told his eager listeners, "Perhaps, when statutes that now create life insurance companies were passed . . . the lawmakers were influenced by the public domain image then prevailing in regard to the life insurance industry. No one seriously looked upon a life insurance charter as a commercial instrument. Perhaps the lawmakers never intended that the life insurance corporation be a commercial vehicle . . . perhaps it was their intention that a life insurance company be quasi public domain . . . non-profit motivated . . . bordering on a benevolent, church-like structure. But what they may have intended to create in their legislation . . . and what they actually did create . . . are vastly different. . . . Long-gone is that image of the benevolent . . . sanctimonious institution which heretofore was public domain in [the businessman's] eyes. He sees it as an instrument of profit."

Only twenty-five years apart were those appraisals made, a quarter of a century that witnessed the emergence of a few thousand new life insurance companies, the holding company device, and previously undreamed-of diversifications, all products of a system with the seeds of ugliness—the system of stock ownership of life insurance companies.[76]

---

[76] The author dealt with the subject of new company proliferation more extensively in an earlier book, *The Case Against* New *Insurance Companies,* Farnsworth Publishing Co., Inc., 1966.

Chapter 4 *Anatomy of Mutualization*

Fundamental to the whole issue of mutualization is the concept of American life insurance as either quasi-public or just plain "business." Viewed in the latter sense, intensive regulation of the life insurance business is no more valid than intensive regulation of the shoe business. Yet our history clearly reveals that in life insurance regulation, the prerogatives of management have been subordinated to the public interest, while the shoe business, except for antitrust restrictions and labor relations (both irrelevant in the context of this discussion), has been left to its own devices. It does not require licensing as a business operation, nor are its salesmen subject to regulatory authority. It does not have to maintain statutory reserves, nor are its management judgments officially reviewed.

Yet, on and on go the contentions that life insurance is just "another business." Surely documentation of such repetition would belabor the point. But citing merely one, may clarify it.

Mehr and Osler wrote in the foreword to their book, *Modern Life Insurance:*

> We have sought to analyze the life insurance business in the terms of the structure of every business or industry. We have treated it as neither saint nor pariah—and to those within the business who would prefer it be referred to as an "institution" and explained as something different and apart from other business, we say that much of the demagogic misunderstanding of life insurance arises from past attempts to set life insurance apart from American business as a whole.

On the other hand, Joseph B. MacLean wrote: "Life insurance companies are totally different in their nature from ordinary commercial corporations formed for profit. The business of life insurance, whether conducted on the stock or on the mutual plan, is fundamentally a cooperative one." [77]

> The business of life insurance is so important in personal financial planning and is such a vital force in the American economy that the responsibilities of life insurance company management extend far beyond those in most other types of business. [78]

Spencer L. Kimball, professor of law, University of Michigan, and one of the country's outstanding authorities on insurance regulation, wrote:

> If socialization of risk is viewed as an objective of insurance regulation, it at once alters the basic focus of the enterprise from one essentially private (albeit subject to control in the public interest) to one which is essentially public, permitted to exist in private form only to the extent that it fulfills society's demands. Despite all our predilections to the contrary, it seems a fact that the basic focus of

---

[77] *Life Insurance,* seventh edition.

[78] *Participating Life Insurance Sold by Stock Companies,* Joseph M. Belth.

the enterprise is changing—subtly and gradually, but inexorably—and the new and pervasive demands of society are becoming more influential.[79]

In his conclusion, Professor Kimball wrote: "Finally, as the insurance enterprise becomes more and more crucial to the social fabric and as regulation acquires more sophistication, the manifold purposes of society at large come to have more and more implications for the process of insurance regulation.[80]

In 1965, at the peak of the new stock life insurance proliferation, William E. Timmons, Iowa Insurance Commissioner, and then president of the National Association of Insurance Commissioners, said,

> I firmly believe that no one has an unqualified right to start a life insurance company. . . . To me, the life insurance business is a special kind of business. It requires the highest morality of its leaders. Each member of the management team must have broad experience, must demonstrate great strength of character, and have the kind of integrity that always puts the interests of policyholders first. The leader of a well-run life insurance company is a special breed of man who has become what he is because he understands and carefully guards the trust that has been put in his hands.[81]

It seems to me to be not a decade late, but a century late, to contend that the life insurance business is not "something different and apart from other business." The mutualization of stock life insurance companies in America, the story of which follows, proves the uniqueness of the life insurance business.

THE MECHANICS OF MUTUALIZATION

As I have pointed out, the mutualization of stock life insurance companies in America is not new either in concept or in fact. It

---

[79] *The Purpose of Insurance Regulation,* Spencer L. Kimball.

[80] Ibid.

[81] American Life Convention Annual Meeting, Toronto, October 23, 1965.

will be recalled that practically all of a stock company's assets—policy reserves and surplus funds—have been created by the policyholders, and that the amount of capital stock, no matter how important in the early years, is of little significance compared with total assets or total liabilities. The outstanding example of this disparity is the previously mentioned situation that existed in the Prudential at the time mutualization proceedings were begun in 1914. The initial capitalization, while $100,000, included only $91,000 paid in cash. All subsequent increases in capitalization were accomplished through the transfer of funds from the surplus account.

Theoretically, the mechanics of mutualization are simple. It is accomplished through the purchase of the capital stock by the policyholders. "The funds required for such a purpose are taken from the general surplus funds of the company when they are sufficient to provide the price acceptable to the stockholders and to leave an adequate contingency fund for the protection of the policyholders. Payments to the stockholders may be spread over a period of years.[82]

THE VALUE OF THE STOCK

Some, perhaps, may question whether the amount necessary to reimburse stockholders would jeopardize the guarantees made to policyholders. Such a situation is unlikely, for if the surplus were that meager, the stock would necessarily have little value. Moreover, since payments to stockholders may be spread over a period of years, the opportunity exists to increase surplus. When mutualization is clearly in the public interest, the authorities, after establishing a fair price for the stock, might arrange a take-over by a more affluent mutual company.

There have been twenty mutualizations in America since the first mutualization law was enacted by New York in 1906—directly

---

[82] *Life Insurance,* seventh edition, Joseph B. MacLean.

following the Armstrong Investigation. (The only prior one was the Phoenix Mutual of Connecticut, begun in 1889 and completed ten years later.) These are the companies, listed chronologically: [83]

Company	State	Mutualization Begun	Completed
Metropolitan	New York	1914	1915
Prudential	New Jersey	1914	1943
Home Life	New York	1916	1916
Equitable	New York	1917	1925
Central Life	Iowa	1919	1919
Provident Mutual	Pennsylvania	1921	1922
Guardian Life	New York	1924	1945
Standard	Oregon	1929	1929
Shenandoah	Virginia	1934	1955
General American	Missouri	1936	1946
National Guardian	Wisconsin	1936	1949
Bankers Life	Nebraska	1941	1949
Ohio National	Ohio	1941	1959
Union Central	Ohio	1941	1954
Pan-American	Louisiana	1943	1952
Federal Life	Illinois	1945	1962
Pacific Mutual	California	1946	1959
Western and Southern	Ohio	1946	1948
Farmers and Traders	New York	1954	Uncompleted
Midland Mutual	Ohio	1955	1956

---

[83] "Motivations Underlying Mutualization of Stock Life Insurance Companies," Linda Pickthorne Fletcher, *Journal of Risk and Insurance,* March 1966.

93

MOTIVATIONS FOR MUTUALIZATION

Dr. Fletcher, formerly assistant professor of insurance in the Wharton School of the University of Pennsylvania, and now associate professor at Louisiana State University, lists four motivations for mutualization: (1) alleviation of adverse public opinion; (2) elimination of potential estate tax problems (of large stockholders); (3) prevention of control of the company from passing to non-company interests, and (4) elimination of operational difficulties.

These motivations, we are informed, "have been observed." A fifth, not yet observed, is the premise of this book—to eliminate the bootless waste of policyholders' money that redounds, unnecessarily, to the exclusive benefit of stockholders.

As far as the past is concerned, we may eliminate Dr. Fletcher's second motivation because of its limited applicability. Her third, while important historically, is not now likely to materialize, except in new or comparatively new companies. The fourth, the elimination of operational difficulties, is, of course, ever present—that is to say, the existence of the difficulties is ever present. In established companies, however, actual control is in the hands of an extremely small number of stockholders, who themselves (or their heirs or relatives) comprise the management team, and who solve, or simply muddle through, their operational problems.

What is left is public opinion, which is or should be synonymous with public interest, and is fundamental to the author's thesis. The three major mutualizations in American life insurance history—those of the Metropolitan, Prudential, and Equitable—were traceable almost exclusively to public opinion, aroused at the revelations brought forth by the Armstrong Committee in 1905. The three companies, then the largest in the world, were the major targets of the investigation. Their indiscretions led to the widespread belief that stockholders' control was incompatible with the fiduciary nature of a life insurance company. As I have previously pointed out, this was unmistakably implied in the Committee's report.

A brief analysis of the mechanics of the three mutualizations is most revealing:

THE METROPOLITAN MUTUALIZATION

The original capitalization was only $200,000, half of which was retired during the 1870s. In 1883, however, capitalists invested an additional $400,000, bringing the company's total stock to $500,000. That remained unchanged, although its capital was later increased to $2 million by a transfer of $1.5 million from surplus. (The company's surplus rose from $6,000 in 1877 to over $13 million in 1904, thus providing a thick cushion for the transfer.) The Metropolitan president, Knapp, held over $700,000 in stock at his retirement in 1891, and his successor, Hegeman, had $275,000 of the company's final capitalization of $2 million. Knapp's shares, over 28,000, paid him annual dividends of almost $50,000.

The stock insurer charter restricted (as did the Equitable's and the Prudential's) the dividend rate to 7 percent of capital. Thus, $140,000 was set aside each year on the total capitalization of $2 million (of which only $500,000 had been invested by stockholders). This represented an annual return of 28 percent.

Such profits, together with high executive salaries, nepotism, speculation in stock and other business ventures, quite naturally resulted in the public's desire for mutualization. In 1914 when those proceedings began, the Metropolitan held admitted assets of close to $448 million, and had in force $2.816 billion of life insurance. The cost of mutualization was $6 million.

THE EQUITABLE MUTUALIZATION

While this mutualization got under way in 1917, the movement actually began in 1911 when the New York Superintendent of Insurance made public a voting trust agreement between J. P. Morgan, owner of the controlling stock, and three trustees. The superintendent approved of the arrangement "pending the ascertainment of a legal means whereby the Equitable . . . be made a mutual company . . ." The "means" was a bill introduced in the legislature that had the approval of the Committee on Mutualization and of the trustees of the Morgan stock. The bill became law in May 1911.

Delays followed, caused chiefly by the destruction of the home office by fire. In June 1915, T. Coleman du Pont purchased 564 shares from the estate of J. P. Morgan and almost immediately thereafter informed the state superintendent that he wished to cooperate in the mutualization. Two years later, an agreed-upon plan was approved by the Equitable board, under which the Equitable would purchase the controlling block of 501 shares at $5,400 each, and the remaining sixty-three shares at $1,500 each, to be paid for with interest, in forty semiannual installments of $111,537.46 each. The only criticism of the plan, according to the superintendent, was the large price paid for the majority shares, the par value of which was only $50,100. He said "these sales indicate that great financiers have recognized the enormous value in the majority stock solely because of its power to control nearly $600,000,000 of trust funds and the effect of such control upon other financial institutions. The removal of this power of control, which at present may be exercised by a single individual, is, to my mind, a sufficient justification for the payment of a higher price for the dominating stock interest than the holding of the minority, even if such payment were to be made directly from the present surplus of the Society." All but twenty-three shares of the minority stock were turned in by May 14, 1918, the deadline fixed by the purchase agreement. The last of the shares were not acquired until 1925, although the Equitable in fact had become a mutual company in 1915.

When mutualization proceedings began the Equitable had admitted assets of $562.4 million, and a total of $1.6 billion insurance in force.[84]

---

[84] The facts surrounding the three mutualizations were gleaned from *The Life Insurance Enterprise, 1885–1910,* Morton Keller; *The Private Insurance Business in the United States Economy,* Nelli and Marshall, Bureau of Business and Economic Research, June 1969; *Best's Insurance Reports.*

THE PRUDENTIAL MUTUALIZATION

The highlights of the mutualization of the Prudential were presented in the opening paragraphs of this book. The only facts to be added are that the original capitalization of $91,000 in cash, was increased through transfers from the surplus account (created, of course, by the policyholders) to $149,000 in 1885; to $208,300 in 1887; to $418,000 in 1889; and finally to $2 million in 1893. The 7 percent restriction on capital, $140,000, amounted to an annual return of 159 percent on the $91,000 actually invested by stockholders.

The last legal action by minority stockholders wasn't settled until 1943, twenty-nine years after the mutualization process began.

Chapter 5 Stocking a Mutual

There have been instances of mutual life insurance companies converting to the stock structure. This has been appropriately referred to as "stocking a mutual." Since the 1930s, none has done so. But previous to those years, they compiled quite a record. This is it:

Central Life Assurance Society in 1902
Reserve Loan Life Insurance Company in 1909
Midland National Life Insurance Company in 1909
Franklin Life in 1910
Peoples Life Insurance Company in 1910
Eureka-Maryland Assurance Corporation in 1918
American Reserve Life Insurance Company in 1925
National Equity Life Insurance Company in 1927

> Monumental Life of Maryland in 1928
> Northwestern National in 1928
> Pyramid Life Insurance Company in 1928
> Farmers' Union Mutual in 1933
> National Old Line Life in 1930
> Republic National Life in 1930
> St. Louis Mutual in 1931
> Texas Mutual Reserve Life in 1935
> Illinois Bankers Life in 1936

Of these seventeen companies, eight converted within four years of their formation. It is reasonable to assume, then, that the stock structure was their original target. Eight have disappeared for one reason or another. One, the Central Life Assurance Society, reverted to mutual in 1919. Eight remain operative as stock companies.

SUCCESS FOR WHOM?

Of these, Franklin Life, Republic National, and Northwestern National have been enormously successful—at least for their stockholders. Franklin now has admitted assets of $561 million, after capitalization and paid-in contributory surplus of less than $5 million. Republic National, with a capital investment of less than $6 million, now has assets of over $250 million. (In 1928, when conversion activities began, its assets were slightly over $10,500.) Northwestern National, on the base of capitalization and paid-in contributory surplus of less than $5 million, now forty-two years after "stocking," has assets of about $600 million.

The following chart explains the success of the stockholders at the expense of the policyholders:

The stockholder success of these three companies is mirrored in the twenty-year actual histories of $10,000 Whole Life policies issued in 1950 to males age thirty-five, on both nonparticipating and participating bases, compared with a similar policy issued by the participating Connecticut Mutual.

	Nonparticipating Franklin Life [85]	Nonparticipating Republic National [85]	Nonparticipating Northwestern National [85]	Participating Connecticut Mutual [85]
Gross Annual Premium	223.80	225.20	217.20	279.70
Average Net Annual Premium	223.80	225.20	217.20	169.30
20 Premiums	4,476.00	4,504.00	4,344.00	3,385.00
20th Year Cash Value	3,230.00	3,230.00	3,520.00	3,624.40
20 Year Net Cost	1,246.00	1,274.00	824.00	GAIN 239.40

	Participating Franklin Life [86]	Participating Republic National	Participating Northwestern National [86]	Participating Connecticut Mutual [86]
Gross Annual Premium	286.00	FIGURES	267.60	279.70
Average Net Annual Premium	215.40	NOT	200.10	169.30
20 Premiums	4,307.50	AVAILABLE	4,002.40	3,385.00
20th Year Cash Value	3,230.20		3,604.90	3,624.40
20 Year Net Cost	1,077.30		397.50	GAIN 239.40

[85] *Flitcraft Compend 1950.*
[86] *Flitcraft Compend 1970.*

A THROWBACK TO DAYS BEST FORGOTTEN

Although no mutual-to-stock conversions have been effected in some thirty years, there is now a resurgence of talk, if not activity, in that direction. The reasons are not difficult to spot. "The mutual that converts to a stock corporate form would be then in a position to effect . . . a parent holding company reorganization [which] would control most or all of the stock of the principal operating insurer and any of its diversified operating subsidiaries." [87] What is desired is "greater perimissiveness" [88] from traditional regulatory control.

While the great mutual companies have been placed at a disad-- vantage by this "permissiveness" granted stock companies in their diversification hijinks, "the prime candidate for conversion [seems] to be the smaller mutual company that wants to expand, but finds it difficult to do so solely by writing increased amounts of insurance or by seeking to acquire additional capital by traditional meth-- ods." [89]

Whatever the motivations for this renewed interest in "stocking a mutual," it is clear that the recent diversification machinations of stock life insurance companies have placed mutual company management on the defensive. The mutuals, being policyholder- oriented, are being pushed hard by the diversifications (holding companies, conglomerates, and other strange adventures) of the stockholder-oriented stock companies.

A PROBLEM FOR THE ECONOMIST OR THE PSYCHIATRIST?

The real motivations, however, for the sudden (but limited) interest in transforming a mutual into a stock company, may lie

---

[87] American Management Association Seminar, Summer 1969.

[88] Ibid.

[89] Ibid.

elsewhere. They may, perhaps, be of a personal nature. You may recall that the New York State Insurance Superintendent, in analyzing the motives of those obsessed with the virtues of the holding company device, said, "[Some men] wanted to use the resources of their insurance companies—to achieve more profit and honor than they foresaw in the conventional enterprise." To support this view, he pointed to the "drama of takeovers, the legerdemain of growth by acquisition, the daredevilry of leverage, and the barbarities of corporate plunder."

Mr. Stewart's perceptive analysis was seconded some months later by Thomas P. Bowles, Jr., of Bowles and Tillinghast, a consulting firm of national repute, whose services had been purchased by many life insurance companies. Mr. Bowles, Jr., said, "Being really honest with themselves, some life insurance executives will admit that the conglomerate's, the congeneric's, the holding company's promise of a better world is exciting because it provides some relief from the boredom of an inadequate, unsatisfying performance in the major responsibility of managing a life insurance company."

Carter H. Golembe, a Washington economic consultant, and an expert on bank regulation, wrote, in connection with one-bank holding companies (basically similar to the life insurance pattern), "For the first time, banking held out the prospect of excitement, of challenge, of a glittering future. . . . Rather than remaining content with an increasingly limited role in the financial spectrum . . . progressive and aggressive bankers had found a way to operate in new and challenging areas of finance."

These authoritative observations suggest that the exponents of diversification in life insurance and banking may not be motivated by the so-called demands of a changing world, but rather by their own restlessness and need for new challenges and excitement. Perhaps, in their fashion, they are simply reflecting the frustrations that are evident in many people, in many places.

While such personal reactions may be sufficient to lead an individual businessman into unorthodox practices, with consequences confined to himself and his family, they are hardly justifiable moti-

103

vations for actions, the results of which threaten the welfare of hundreds of thousands—indeed challenge the wholesomeness of an entire quasi-public institution.

In any event, the change from mutual ownership to stockholder ownership is destined to effect a change in management philosophy from policyholder orientation to stockholder orientation—and that is the root of the thesis of this book.

THE MONUMENTAL LIFE CAPER

To bring it into full focus, let us turn to the hearings and report of the Temporary National Economic Committee, appointed in 1939 to explore the subject of concentrated economic power, and the last investigation in which life insurance was even indirectly involved. We learn that "the recent history of the Monumental Life Insurance Company of Baltimore, Maryland, provides an example of the manner in which the directors of a mutual company may take control from the policyholders by changing its form to a stock company." [90]

And what an example! To accomplish "the stocking," a "cryptic note sufficient only to meet statutory requirements, was placed in 2 Baltimore newspapers, notifying the policyholders of a meeting to be held . . . to vote on the conversion plan. No published notice was given outside of the city of Baltimore, although 30% of the company's business was outside Baltimore, and only 2 of the company's 27 branch offices were located in that city." [91]

Since the company's policyholders (who actually owned the company) could not be expected to attend the meeting, and indeed were not enthusiastically invited, their proxies were essential for "stocking the mutual." Each of the thousand company agents was

---

[90] Monograph No. 28, "The Study of Legal Reserve Life Insurance Companies" made under the auspices of the Securities and Exchange Commission for the Temporary National Economic Committee, July 1940.

[91] Ibid.

given ten dollars to obtain proxies. "The form of proxy used, in addition to containing authority (for the directors) to vote for the conversion itself, contained a provision whereby policyholders were asked to waive the rights guaranteed them under the Maryland statute to subscribe to stock of the new company." [92]

For ten dollars each, the agents of the company (most of them didn't know what was up) secured sufficient proxies to effect the conversion from mutual to stock. The methods used were highly questionable, to put it charitably. "Testimony obtained from agents of the company indicated serious irregularities . . ." [93]

The distribution of the stock of the new company was dramatically revealing. "Only 3 policyholders who were not employed by the company, or connected in some way with its management, received any shares of stock." [94] Two of them were granted five shares each, and the other a hundred shares, of a total of five thousand.

Because many branch managers and employees were unable to take up their subscriptions (an eventuality that conceivably may have been anticipated), five officers and directors wound up with the vast majority of available shares. Within a few years, the group that conceived and carried out the conversion plan (stocking a mutual) received almost $600,000 in cash dividends, and the company, then owned largely by them, had a surplus of $2 million. "Stock dividends of $1 million each in 1934, 1944, 1949, 1952 and 1955, $2 million in 1958 and 1961, $2.5 million in 1964 (concurrently the shares were split 2 for 1 reducing the par value to $5) and $2.5 million in 1967 raised capital to $15 million. In early 1968 plans were announced that the company will purchase either in the open market or in direct transaction up to 10% of its outstanding shares." [95]

---

[92] Ibid.

[93] Ibid.

[94] Ibid.

[95] *Best's Life Insurance Reports, 1969.*

THE ILLINOIS BANKERS LIFE CAPER

The other mutual-to-stock conversion investigated by the SEC for the TNEC was the Illinois Bankers Life of Monmouth, Illinois. The machinations of this one were far too involved for simple reporting. But the committee's report sums it up in unequivocal terms:

> Thus, in summary, it appears that a group of policyholders owned a life insurance company with assets of approximately $8,000,000. Mr. Hugh T. Martin, an officer of that company, decided to take control away from the policyholders and to place himself in the dominant position. Some of his fellow officers hesitated to join him in this venture. He bought their cooperation for about $300,000. A new company was organized to take over the assets and after an inequitable reinsurance plan was consummated, Mr. Martin used the funds of the company to satisfy obligations incurred in the payments to his fellow officers, and even to finance in part the stock which he owned in the company. Finally, a rewriting contract was engineered through which policyholders, partially by misrepresentation, were persuaded to transfer their policies on a basis which was inequitable and at a price which was padded to the amount of approximately $10 a policyholder in order that a fund of $430,000 might be diverted for Mr. Martin's personal benefit. The sum was sufficient to satisfy all obligations incurred in acquiring the company and Mr. Martin thus was placed in the position of controlling approximately $8,000,000 without having invested a cent. This position he has continued to occupy. He is both president and principal stockholder of the company today.

This much is certain: the conversion of stock life insurance companies to the mutual form is unquestionably to the benefit of the policyholders. The reverse conversion is a promise, if not a guarantee, of profit to the stockholders.

A CAPER SCOTCHED?

The most recent attempt, characterized by some as landmark, to convert from mutual to stock, occurred in Wisconsin between

March 1969 and April 1970. The Hardware Dealers Mutual Fire Insurance Company had, as a subsidiary, the Sentry Corporation, a holding company, owning several firms affiliated with the Hardware Mutuals organization. The Sentry Group embraced twenty-three companies, including the Sentry Life Insurance Company. The issue was a proposal to convert the Hardware Dealers from mutual to stock, and place it under the ownership of its subsidiary, to be called the Sentry Insurance Company. The move, according to the *Milwaukee Journal* of March 31, 1969, "will be another case of the child adopting the parent."

Success of the plan depended on a two-thirds approval vote by the Fire company's policyholders, and the approval of the Wisconsin Insurance Department. The Sentry Corporation was to be set up with 400,000 shares of $25.00 par value common stock and 3,000,000 shares of $5.00 par value preferred stock. Policyholders of the mutual were to receive cash or stock on a pro-rated basis according to the amounts they had paid in premiums.

The vice-president and general counsel of the Hardware Mutuals said the conversion of the Fire company from mutual to stock would be one of the biggest switchovers in insurance history; that it would pave the way for diversification, for access to the capital market, and for a better competitive position. The Fire company had reported a net loss of almost $3 million in 1968 against a profit of $1.3 million in 1967. Through the medium of a holding company, it was claimed, some of the up-and-down conditions of the fire and casualty business could be avoided.

The president of the Hardware Mutuals, in a letter to the Fire company's policyholders, said that the advantages of the proposed new structure had already been recognized by other large insurance groups. The proxy statement in citing such organizations, admitted that they had previously been stock companies.

Shortly after the announcement of the proposal, Bernard L. Webb, who had previously been a marketing and actuarial specialist for the Sentry Group, and was then a professor of insurance at Georgia State University, wrote to the comptroller general and insurance commissioner of Georgia, warning of "a potentially dangerous situation," and contending that the terms were "not equitable to the company's policyholders." He spelled his conclusions out in considerable detail. The Georgia commissioner sent a copy of the Webb letter to the Wisconsin insurance commissioner urging him to give serious study "to the inequities of the stock purchase plan."

The author of the letter also communicated with the SEC, complaining about "probable violation of the federal securities laws and regulations. . . ." He criticized the accounting procedure that showed the 1968 net loss of almost $3 million.

According to the *Milwaukee Journal* of December 10, 1969, "It was learned here that the insurance commissioners of some other states were concerned about the large increase in Hardware Dealers' loss reserves which could eventually be a multi-million-dollar benefit to the stockholders of the firm."

At that time, the Senate subcommittee headed by Senator Hart was investigating the Hardware Fire switchover in connection with its automobile insurance probe. The senator had retained Webb as a special consultant in the Sentry matter in June 1969.

The events were described this way by Jack Anderson in his syndicated column of March 10, 1969: [96] "The Webb report blows the lid off a scheme . . . to convert Hardware Dealers Mutual . . . into a stock company. This would have transferred control of the mutual company from the 341,500 policyholders to [two insiders] and 31 of their pals. . . . All told, the 33 stood to make a $10 million bonanza at the expense of the policyholders." In the same column, Anderson wrote, "[Senator] Hart cautioned that if the coup succeeded in Wisconsin it would open the floodgates to similar takeovers, costing millions of insured Americans hundreds of millions of dollars."

The Webb report was released at the intervention of Senator Proxmire, chairman of the key financial institutions subcommittee. According to the *Milwaukee Journal* of December 13, 1969, the senator "and his staff experts . . . pegged the amount of the po-

---

[96] Repeated substantially on May 7, 1970.

tential windfall to the management group at the expense of the 341,500 company policyholders at an even higher figure—$16.5 million."

After the Webb report had bounced around from one committee to another, a hearing was conducted by the Wisconsin insurance commissioner on December 18, 1969. The previous day, however, had brought forth a modification of the original switchover plan. Presumably as the result of testimony at the hearing, Webb, as reported by the *Milwaukee Sentinel,* "apologized all around and said he had accomplished what he set out to do." He said he would revise his report in Washington and Madison (Wisconsin) in accordance with the facts brought out at the hearing. The *Sentinel* quoted Webb as having said, "I wish it [the company's change of position] had been achieved with less blood and tears. . . . The result was about what I originally wanted," referring apparently to the company's revised proposal to distribute all of Hardware Dealers' $24 million equity to policyholders in common stock.

The modified stock reorganization plan was rejected by the Wisconsin insurance commissioner a few months after the hearings (a second one had been held in February 1970). His reason, a technical one, was based on a state law that did not permit conversion of a mutual insurance company into a noninsurance corporation.

The commissioner, however, according to the Journal Company, April 7, 1970, made these points that were basic to the fundamental issue:

> Although the stated reason for reorganization—the growth in capital for needed expansion—was valid, the record did not disclose any plan to provide additional capital.
>
> The record was not convincing that additional diversification of investments available to Sentry would have any beneficial impact on the growth and profitability of Hardware Dealers.
>
> The transfer of assets from a sister company, Hardware Mutual Casualty Co., to Hardware Dealers endangered the interest of the Hardware Mutual policyholders because the assets were turned over at less value.

Certainly relevant to the subject of this book were these additional observations of the Wisconsin insurance commissioner:

> Management that operates both a mutual and a stock company engaged in the same business is vulnerable to charges of conflict of interest in its attempt to operate a stock insurance company and a holding company complex in the interest of profit for stockholders while, on the other hand, operating a mutual casualty insurance company in the interest of policyholders. . . . These are inconsistent purposes and there is no question but that loyalties would tend toward one side of the complex at the expense of the other. . . .

If the transformation from mutual to stock promised to benefit only the policyholders, it is hardly conceivable that it would ever be attempted.

The history of "stockings" constitutes, it seems to me, a sharp castigation of the stock structure itself.

Chapter **6** *The Anomaly—*
Stock Company
Participating Policies

For reasons that escape me, the advocates of stock company life insurance don't merely prefer that type to the mutual coverage; they bitterly resent the mutuals. And their resentment is focused on dividends. Thus many of them simply assume that all mutual companies sell participating policies, and stock companies sell only nonparticipating contracts. This is clearly evident in the books they write.

James E. Stowers made this puerile statement in his book, *Why Waste Your Money . . . On Life Insurance?:*

The two basic types of life insurance companies are:
1. The mutual company which issues participating policies.
2. The stock company which issues nonparticipating policies.

111

An equally puerile statement appears in *How to Avoid Being Overcharged by Your Life Insurance Salesman* by J. Edward Pawlick.

> All mutual life insurance companies charge more than they need to pay death claims. . . . Then they give some back to you at the end of the year. They call these "dividends." . . . The non-mutual companies, which are not cooperatives but are corporations owned by stockholders . . . are able to charge lower rates right at the beginning. They don't over-charge and then give some money back.

Frank S. J. McIntosh describes dividends in his *A Study of Mutual Life Insurance Dividends* as "deception," "black magic," "crystal gazing," and "not to be relied on." Embarrassingly enough, he wrote "the mutual system of life insurance outrages all the tenants [sic] of true democracy."

The books I've mentioned are all rather recent. Back in 1936, M. and E. A. Gilbert in their book, *Life Insurance—A Legalized Racket,* described dividends as "the mutual myth."

The Mortality Merchants by G. Scott Reynolds, written only a few years ago, observed:

> Law requires that mutual life insurance companies sell only "participating" insurance, and "participating" insurance requires a needless overcharge—even on pure term policies—in order that "dividends" (rebates) may be paid. Therefore, do not—under any circumstances—consider buying your pure death protection from a mutual company.

All these books, and others of the same ilk, have been read by thousands of stock company representatives, some of whom have undoubtedly been led to believe that "stock company" and "nonparticipating" are synonymous.

THE STOCK COMPANIES SELL BOTH KINDS

To the dismay of many of these fanatical dividend haters, and to the horror of some, most of the largest and most respected stock companies sell dividend-paying or participating policies, in addition to the nonparticipating type. In fact, almost 25 percent of all stock company ordinary [97] business in force participates in dividends.

But the stock companies came to sell participating policies years after their incorporation. Lincoln National, for example, began operations in 1905 and first sold participating life insurance in 1931. Franklin Life, incorporated as a stock company in 1910, did not sell participating policies until 1940. Continental Assurance, formed in 1911, sold only nonparticipating insurance during the next twenty-six years.

WILL THE REAL REASON PLEASE STAND UP?

Why did those companies, and many other stock companies, enter the participating field? After all, the nonparticipating type produces greater profits for the stockholders. A comparison of the two types sold by the same companies readily reveals this. The following figures are based on the actual histories of $10,000 Whole Life policies issued in 1950 to men age thirty-five:

	Nonparticipating Annual Premiums	Average Net Annual Premiums Participating Policies
Aetna	$222.40	$190.90
Connecticut General	222.40	191.70
Equitable of Iowa	225.50	202.40
Franklin Life	223.80	215.40
Lincoln National	224.90	not available
Continental Assurance	221.40	196.00

The guaranteed twentieth year cash values were the same for the two types in three of the companies. The other three guaranteed an average of $277 *more* to the participating policyholder.

---

[97] Exclusive of group and credit insurance.

The lower cost of the participating policies in the same company results from design, not accident. About five years ago, the president of a large stock company said, "It is a definite objective of our Company to provide over a substantial period better results to our participating policyholders than to nonparticipating policyholders, since the former are in effect sharing in the risks of fluctuations in interest earnings, mortality, and expenses, and we feel they should receive definite benefit from this risk-sharing." [98] (Results over decades prove that such risk is almost nonexistent.)

An interesting sidelight was the experience of a stock company some years ago. Selling only nonparticipating insurance, the agents found themselves at a serious competitive disadvantage. Their pleas to management resulted in the introduction of several participating contracts. These were so favorably viewed by prospective buyers that top management joined with the agents in encouraging the sale of the participating policies. Continued success was a major factor in the mutualization of the company a few years later. [99]

To become competitive with the mutual companies, then, is beyond doubt the primary motivation of the stock companies that entered the participating field. Actual dividend histories, as well as projections of current dividend scales, both readily available to agents (and hence their prospects) illustrate the great cost superiority of participating policies. That this is recognized by the insurance-buying public is evident from the fact that well over 70 percent of all ordinary [100] life insurance in force is participating, of which only about 11½ percent is in stock companies. To get a greater share of new insurance, it seems that the stock companies must sell participating policies. Moreover to recruit agents, and to keep them, stock companies are practically forced into the participating field.

---

[98] *Participating Life Insurance Sold by Stock Companies,* Joseph M. Belth.

[99] "Motivations Underlying the Mutualization of Stock Life Insurance Companies," Linda Pickthorne Fletcher in the March 1966 issue of the *Journal of Risk and Insurance.*

[100] Exclusive of group, industrial, and credit insurance.

STOCKHOLDERS VS. POLICYHOLDERS

This anomalous situation has led to a serious conflict of interests between stockholders, who expect periodic distributions from surplus, and policyholders, who are led to believe that they will receive, in the form of annual dividends, the unused safety margins that were included in their premiums.

This problem has been recognized by some of the state regulatory authorities, and by company officials as well. In 1962, Howard C. Reeder, then president of the Continental Assurance Company of Chicago (a stock company selling both participating and nonparticipating policies), drew a proper distinction. After stating that individual nonparticipating insurance is the most desirable from the stockholders' viewpoint, he said, "Since the higher premium received on participating business furnishes a cushion against adverse experience which practically removes all stockholders' risk on such contracts, a limit on profits, therefore, whether self-imposed or required by law, seems entirely proper."

A limited number of states have imposed a ceiling on the portion of the profits on participating policies that may benefit the stockholders. While such a limitation is right and proper, it is clear that whatever is allocated to stockholders is not available for distribution to policyholders in the form of dividends. It follows, of course, that participating policyholders in a stock company must pay more for their coverage than the policyholders in a mutual company, who receive all of the unneeded safety margins.

But the statutory limitations on stockholder profit is by no means nationwide. Forty-two states have no law relating to maximum surplus limitations on participating insurance. But even the more enlightened states don't totally prevent abuses. Many stock companies do not apprise their stockholders of the limitation, and in their annual reports to stockholders represent the entire net gain from operations as accruing to the benefit of stockholders. Thus in practically all states either the policyholders or the stockholders, or both, have little clarification of their respective and conflicting interests.

115

A VIEW FROM THE PAST

The problem is not a new one. Back in 1905, the famous Armstrong Committee was deeply concerned with the rights of participating policyholders, and said this in its Report:

> It is manifest that all gains or surplus in excess of such contingent fund [requirements] should, in equity, be returned to the holders of participating policies at such appropriate times as may be practicable for their ascertainment. This return should be effected in such a manner that the policyholders will share in the proportions in which, through their payments, they have contributed to the gains. For this purpose the company owes it to its policyholders to give them at convenient periods a gain and loss exhibit showing the actual results of the company's business, by which the efficiency of the managers may be tested and the amount available for return to the policyholders determined.
>
> Of all the reforms suggested by the Committee nothing, it is believed, is more imperatively demanded than that the companies should be compelled to exhibit the results of their management by annual accounting. If details of management are to be left, as they should be, to the discretion of the directors, they should be compelled each year to state the results of their administration and to come under definite liabilities to the policyholders for the amounts to which the latter are entitled.

The Committee recognized the problems inherent in a company selling both participating and nonparticipating policies and felt that such a dual operation should not be permitted. The resulting New York law prohibited domestic mutual and stock companies writing participating business from writing the nonparticipating type. By administrative interpretation, this restriction was extended to out-of-state companies doing business in New York. In 1937 the New York Insurance Department ruled that such out-of-state companies could issue both types of life insurance, provided that they submit separate profit-and-loss statements, and that all profits on participating business had to inure to such policyholders. The latter restriction was later relaxed by the state legislature and now both domestic and foreign stock companies may issue both kinds, subject to stringent restrictions imposed by the insurance law.

The fundamental issue was brought into even sharper focus by the Armstrong Committee through its suggestion that neither mutual companies nor stock companies issuing participating policies be permitted to write the nonparticipating type. The Report stated:

> . . . mutual companies and stock companies chartered to transact business on the mutual plan or holding themselves out as transacting business on this basis, should be forbidden from writing nonparticipating policies.
>
> The writing of nonparticipating policies by these companies must almost necessarily result in an injustice. If premiums are charged at a rate lower than the actual cost of carrying the insurance, including a fair rate of expenses, it is an imposition upon the other policyholders who must contribute to pay the difference. If, on the other hand, the premiums are at a rate higher than that demanded by the cost of carrying the insurance, the excess is without excuse and those who take the policies are overcharged and are deprived of the returns to which they should be entitled. . . .

It is abundantly clear that participation by policyholders in a stock life insurance company should not be left entirely to the discretion of the board of directors that elects the management team. In mutual companies, the policyholders, as sole owners, are entitled to elect directors. In stock companies, neither participating nor nonparticipating policyholders possess this right. Such boards are elected by the stockholders, and they, and they alone, have the power to determine the dividends to be paid to the participating policyholders. Moreover, stockholders, quite naturally, desire ever-increasing earnings, and an increasing surplus account to enhance the value of their shares.

THE DIVISION IS NOT EXPLAINED

In the majority of states, the problem is compounded by virtue of the fact that companies writing both participating and nonparticipating policies are not required to furnish separate gain-and-loss exhibits for each class. This permissiveness contrasts sharply with the requirement that companies writing either participating or non-participating policies exclusively must submit clear-cut gain-and-loss exhibits. It is apparent that "a gain or loss exhibit which combines both classes winds up by not disclosing the results for either class." [101]

To remedy this extremely loose situation, some state insurance commissioners in 1960 requested the Blanks Committee of the National Association of Insurance Commissioners to include a provision in company annual statements for a complete separation of accounts. The treatment of that suggestion over the following three years provides us with special insight into the inherent dangers to the public of stockholder-orientation of life insurance companies.

One would expect that stock companies would, of course, oppose the proposition. Unfortunately, they were joined by most of the mutuals. The two largest and most influential company associations —The American Life Convention and The Life Insurance Association of America—both composed of mutual and stock companies, expressed their opposition. Why the mutuals that clearly recognized the advisability of separate account reporting, and stood to benefit competitively from its adoption, joined the opposition is a matter of conjecture. One motivation may have been the desire to continue the spirit of friendly rivalry rather than to risk an institutional parting of the ways. Another might have been the fear of reprisals of one kind or another. In any event, the only mutual company that opposed the ALC and LIAA, and came out openly for the complete separation of accounts was the Northwestern Mutual, whose Memorandum will form the basis of the discussion that follows.

Before proceeding along those lines, however, it will be helpful to present some of the details of the Blanks Committee meetings. The 1960 proposal required "dual line stock companies to disclose

---

[101] The 1963 Northwestern Mutual Memorandum to the NAIC Blanks Committee.

a complete separation of accounts, including an allocation of the surplus accounts, as a part of their regular annual statement." Because of industry opposition, that portion of the proposal which would have required an allocation of the surplus accounts was withdrawn, and further consideration of the remainder of the proposal was deferred until the following year.

"In 1961, the proposal for a partial separation of accounts, not including a provision for allocation of the surplus accounts, was reintroduced. Again, because of industry opposition, it failed to pass. The proposal was carried forward to the agenda for the 1962 meeting of the Life Subcommittee of the Blanks Committee but was withdrawn prior to the meeting. The proposal was reintroduced in 1963 but was defeated by a vote of eight to seven. . . . The proposal was reintroduced in 1964 but was defeated ten to five. . . ."[102] Since that time, no action has been taken, nor has there been any public discussion. Separate accounts for participating and nonparticipating insurance in stock companies has become a dead issue.

WE'VE HEARD IT BEFORE

A careful analysis of the Memorandum of the ALC and LIAA opposing the proposal of a "partial" separation of accounts reveals a strange similarity to the opposition of many manufacturers of food products to the proposed truth-in-packaging bill. The public, many of them claim, doesn't need such protection; the proposals would further confuse buyers; the proposals would lead to other requirements, all of them costly, and hence lead to price increases; the manufacturers, regardless of contents stated in fractional ounces, and regardless of packages only partially filled with merchandise, are public spirited and therefore should be left to their own devices.

It seems that opposition to price disclosure, regardless of the nature of the products and services involved, almost invariably fol-

---

[102] *Participating Life Insurance Sold by Stock Companies,* Joseph M. Belth.

lows the same line. With minor revisions, a blueprint would serve as the vehicle of all such opposition. Not only, then, is opposition to public information predictable, but its form and content, in a multitude of profit-making endeavors, are strikingly similar.

The joint ALC-LIAA brief was no exception. It argued that the proposed disclosure was "not necessary"; that it "could create problems and lead to misunderstanding"; that management could "determine a fair dividend scale" without it; that the problem "is a matter for management decision"; that there "would be no relationship between the participating earnings . . . and the dividends that a company should in fairness pay"; that information presently provided "is clear and understandable"; that "some 40 states do not require that such an analysis be made or filed"; that the proposal will create "misunderstanding"; that it could "lead to an almost endless multiplication of such separations."

So trite and unimpressive were these defenses, that in a court of law they might very well have led to a directed verdict against their sponsors, without further ado. But since they were made on behalf of almost the entire life insurance industry, and since state regulation of life insurance could be described, on occasion, as regulation by the regulated, the "defenses" were treated with unmerited solemnity.

As I have pointed out, only the Northwestern Mutual kicked up, and, it seems to me, any impartial observer would have recognized that its rebuttal utterly destroyed the contentions made against the proposal.

The Northwestern Mutual maintained that "there is no area in the operation of a company selling participating life insurance where a higher sense of trusteeship to policyholders is required and where full disclosure is more essential."

The Memorandum spelled out the public interest in the matter. "The interest of the participating policyholder in a stock company," it said, "stems from his desire for lower net costs, and these result from dividends as large as possible consistent with safety. Regardless of the reason for the interest of the policyholder—safety or dividends—he ought to be able to make an intelligent determination from the annual statement. If these questions are of natural interest to policyholders of companies which write only one line or the other, are they not of equal interest to policyholders of a company writing both lines?"

THE CONTENTIONS REFUTED

The Northwestern Mutual Memorandum then proceeded to answer each of the ALC-LIAA bromidic, and perhaps tongue-in-cheek, arguments and simply devastated them.

Management, the argument stated, does not need a separate gain-and-loss exhibit to determine a fair dividend scale. "We are not discussing what the management needs," the Northwestern Mutual contended. "We are discussing information which should be available to policyholders of both classes, to stockholders, to the public, and to the officials who regulate our business."

To the argument that "there is no necessary relationship between participating earnings and equitable dividends," the Northwestern responded, ". . . if this argument is valid, it would mean that the whole concept of a gain and loss exhibit should be abandoned. Under this thinking, the business would return to the anarchy which prevailed before the Armstrong Investigation." Moreover, the data under discussion should be "made readily available to every segment of the public. . . . This is the philosophy which our state and federal anti-trust laws were designed to stimulate and encourage. . . . What is the best thing for the public, and what will best insure confidence in the system by which this public business is regulated?"

So the inclusion of separate gain-and-loss exhibits would create misunderstanding. ". . . companies writing one line or the other exclusively," the Northwestern answered, "have dealt with this problem for years; one is prompted to ask, why should companies which write both lines receive what, in effect, is preferential treatment?"

121

Finally, responding to the charge that the proposal could lead to almost endless separations of accounts, the Northwestern pointed to numerous separations that the recent past had necessitated. ". . . the requirement for separate gain and loss exhibits for participating and nonparticipating business," it claimed, "should stand on its own feet, uninfluenced by possible threats about the expansion of the principle into different areas. These can be dealt with if and when they arise."

The Northwestern Mutual Memorandum pulled no punches in its summation in stating:

> Some believe that when the technical arguments are put to one side, the objections to this proposal are due to fear of two things:
>
> (1) The full disclosure of operating results brought about by a separate gain and loss exhibit for participating and nonparticipating business will restrict the freedom of companies writing both of these classes to apportion their income among the various groups at interest.
>
> (2) Full disclosure of separate operating results for each class of business may take away a competitive advantage now enjoyed by companies which publish less revealing figures by co-mingling their results on both classes in a single exhibit. If the proposal were adopted, companies writing participating or nonparticipating business exclusively would be able for the first time to make a direct comparison of their results with the comparable results of companies writing both classes of business.

The Memorandum went on to say, "Ours is a quasi-public business. Those who deal with the funds reported in a gain and loss exhibit are regarded in law as fiduciaries, governed by the highest principles of trusteeship . . . Adoption of the proposal would enable policyholders, stockholders, those who regulate us, and the public at large, to better determine whether we have efficiently and equitably discharged the burdens which the law has placed upon us. To us it seems anomalous for our business to spend millions of dollars in advertising, to create in the public eye a favorable impression of our devotion to the interests of the customer, and at the same time oppose a measure which gives the public a better measure of our performance and stewardship."

The conclusions reached by the Northwestern Mutual and those reached by Joseph M. Belth in his authoritative and comprehensive book, *Participating Life Insurance Sold by Stock Companies,* are strikingly similar and convincing.

Professor Belth concluded as follows:

> In the opinion of the author, inclusion of a complete separation of accounts in the annual statement is the preferable approach. It would seem that the development of a complete separation of accounts for the examiners alone might fail to accomplish adequate public disclosure and might thereby create an undesirable atmosphere of suspicion concerning the disposition of the funds generated by the participating business of the company. At the same time, it would seem that a stock company acting with the utmost good faith toward its stockholders and participating policyholders would have no reason to conceal its actions from public view. Rather, it would seem that such a company would be willing to display its results publicly and defend its actions against any and all criticism.

And then Dr. Belth made these additional observations: ". . . and if any companies are acting with something less than the utmost good faith, it is imperative that the questionable practices of such companies be corrected at the earliest possible date, lest such practices achieve a magnitude that would bring discredit upon the entire institution of life insurance"; ". . . such disclosure requirements are increasingly in demand by some state regulatory officials, federal agencies, security analysts, and even some segments of the life insurance industry itself. In the face of this growing pressure, the vigorous opposition by the regulatory officials of some states to realistic disclosure requirements seems difficult to understand"; "because of the fundamental nature of participating life insurance, it is the author's opinion that stock companies selling participating life insurance should be required to observe strict limitations on the extent to which the stockholders may benefit from participating operations."

123

The failure to adopt the proposed disclosure procedure certainly reflects no credit on the regulatory authorities, the stock companies, and those mutual companies who, for whatever undisclosed reasons, joined the opposition. *The fundamental point, however, is that the structure of stock life insurance companies—and that alone—created the problem and perpetuates it.*

Chapter 7 *Strange Sales Weapons*

Nothing, it seems to me, is more revealing of the undesirability of nonparticipating stock company life insurance than the arguments that have been made in its support.

With the record clearly establishing the fact that mutual life insurance is more advantageous to the policyholder than nonparticipating coverage, the contentions that are made to convince the insurance-buying public that the opposite is true range from merely fallacious to near-demagogic. Let us examine them, followed by refutations.

Argument No. 1—The invested difference between the gross premiums makes the nonparticipating policy a better buy.

Refutation: Not many years ago, the house organ of a stock life insurance company carried the following under the by-line of an assistant vice-president: "Just as a matter of interest I have compared ownership in a mutual life company with true ownership in life insurance companies. I have taken 1941 premiums for $100,000 of Ordinary Life at age 35 from four of the largest mutual companies. The average premium is $2,526. I have done the same with four of the largest stock companies. Their average premium is $1,918, for a difference of $608. The result of investing $100 per year into the Alfred M. Best Life Stock index, starting in 1941 was $32,323 in 1961 for each $100 per year invested. If you multiply this by 6.08 representing the $608 annual difference, the result is really astronomical—$196,000. Using actual dividend histories, accumulated dividends on the mutual company policy come to about $15,500 for the same 20 year period. Now this is what I call ownership in a life insurance company."

Apparently believing that the agents of that company would recite this nonsensical story to their prospects (undoubtedly the hope of its author) the New York State Insurance Department demanded a retraction. Accordingly, the company wrote to all those who had received the original statement, "We regret that the article was misleading and contained inaccuracies which have resulted in controversial discussion and criticism. . . . You are hereby instructed to disregard the article and its contents. . . ." That company's representatives were not, to my knowledge, ever instructed not to make the same kind of argument to their prospects. Ignoring the unreality of using hindsight to predict the future, it is obvious that the annual dividends to the mutual company buyer, exceeding by far the $608 difference in gross premiums, could be or could have been invested in the same fashion as the "difference" was invested. Had it been, the twentieth year accumulation would have been far in excess of the "astronomical" $196,000. Instead, however, of putting the "differences" and the dividends to the same use, the former were hypothetically invested in leaping common stock while the latter accumulated at perhaps 3 percent or 4 percent. The reasoning behind this absurd comparison can be used to prove that it is better to have $90.00 than $100. The $100 in a savings bank will be worth, at 5 percent interest, $105 at the end of one year. The $90.00 invested in a common stock that has a 50 percent rise in market value, will be worth $135 at the end of the year. This is not an inaccurate analogy.

The crazy-quilt argument has been repeated endlessly by agents of stock companies. A few years ago, a stock company agent wrote, in a letter to me, "Considering a male 35 purchasing $10,000 Ordinary Life from both Connecticut Mutual and American National with premiums deducted from a savings account presently earning interest of $3\frac{1}{2}\%$, we obtain a true picture. According to Flitcraft [acknowledged statistical experts] 1968, Connecticut Mutual projects a net gain of $529 after 20 years, while American National has a net cost of $426. We are comparing equals here in the form of level premium permanent life insurance. Comparing equal capital utilization indicates the $39.40 difference in premium will grow to $1,150 in 20 years through the savings account. This alters the picture from a cost of $426 to a gain of $624 versus the $529 gain with Connecticut Mutual." This agent completely ignored the fact that twenty years of Connecticut Mutual dividends exceeded, by a very considerable margin, the $39.40 difference in gross premiums. Worse, he credited the $39.40 differences with $3\frac{1}{2}$ percent compound interest, while crediting the larger Connecticut Mutual dividends with no interest whatever.

This mathematical nonsense has been used by stock company agents for decades. They fail to acknowledge that whatever is done with the gross premium differentials can also be done with the dividends. They credit the latter with 3 percent or 4 percent (or nothing) while accumulating the former at 10 percent or 20 percent, or investing it in the past history of Polaroid.

Argument No. 2—"The policyholder can buy more face value for the same amount of premium under the non-participating plan than he can under the participating plan." [103]

Refutation: This is indeed a strange observation for it ignores completely the dividends on the participating policy. When the

---

[103] *Modern Life Insurance,* Mehr and Osler.

annual refund of the unneeded safety margin is sufficient to bring the net premium for the participating policy under the premium for the nonparticipating policy, which occurs generally in the early policy years, the participating policyholder is the one who has the room for "more face value." For the nonparticipating buyer to purchase more coverage at the outset for the initial difference in going-in outlay would merely compound his disadvantages.

Argument No. 3—Those who have invested their own money are likely to give it their close attention and to provide more efficient management than mutual company management.

Refutation: Both types of companies are controlled by boards of directors. In stock companies the board members are elected by the stockholders; in mutuals by the policyholders. In view of this, it is likely that the operations of a stock company are stockholder oriented, and the operations of a mutual, policyholder oriented. Moreover, it would seem that the policyholders in stock companies should have a reasonable degree of control since "a very large proportion of accumulated funds in an established stock company has been contributed by policyholders and is, *in equity,* the property of the policyholders. The capital stock, if any, is comparatively small in amount. It would therefore appear reasonable that the policyholders should have some voice in management." [104]

Actually, stockholders in electing board members do not exercise the control imputed to them. The stock is too widely dispersed to permit it. It has been authoritatively said that "the dispersion of stock . . . means that to change control, more stockholders must be persuaded, against the advice of management, to vote their stock for someone whom . . . they do not know and will not be disposed to trust. The effort must also contend with the tendency of the indifferent to give proxies to management. . . . And it must contend finally with the alternative, always available to the dissatisfied stockholder, of sim-

---

[104] *Life Insurance,* Joseph B. Maclean.

ply selling his stock. Corporate size, the passage of time, and the dispersion of stock ownership do not disenfranchise the stockholder. Rather, he can vote but his vote is valueless.[105]

It is true that that observation is a general one about all corporations that are publicly owned. But books written specifically about life insurance, by acknowledged students of life insurance, make the same point. Huebner and Black in their book, *Life Insurance,* wrote: "It should be noted that, as in the case of other large national corporations, a [life insurance] stock company with a large number of widely scattered stockholders is controlled by its management group through proxy arrangements."

The Mehr and Osler book, *Modern Life Insurance,* certainly no advocate of mutual companies, includes this strong statement: "Translated into plain language, *stock [life] companies* are often controlled by 2 or 3 officers (or relatives or friends thereof) who own a working majority of the stock. *Mutual companies* are often controlled by a few officers who have a working majority of votes by virtue of owning policies themselves and holding proxies from other policyholders. There is no *practical difference* between the methods of 'control' in a stock [life] insurance company and those in a mutual [life] insurance company."

The argument that stock companies have more interested and capable "control" is simply invalid. What of management efficiency? Among established companies, there is little to choose between the two types of companies. The boards are composed of the same kind of people. The officers are much alike in terms of skill and dedication. Comparatively new stock companies, however, present a different picture. Melvin L. Gold, consulting actuary to a number of new stock companies, wrote, "I have always been struck by the significance of most Boards of Directors. Their prime function seems to be that of glamorizing the prospectus . . . in order to facilitate the sale of stock." [106] About the management skill of executives of new stock life insurance companies, Mr. Gold wrote: "The scarcity

---

105 *The New Industrial State,* John Kenneth Galbraith.

106 *Insurance Gold Book,* September 11, 1965.

of top-notch insurance executives with a broad understanding of the business is appalling. . . . The dearth of personnel has forced companies to play a game of musical chairs with agents and executives. And finding a company president who knows the inherent profit in the policies he is selling is almost like participating in a Ponce de Leon search. New companies are often headed by agents or general agents who . . . hire high-priced agency vice presidents (who always control plenty of business) and then only consider the administration process as an after-thought. As a result, the new companies are generally headed by 'strong' salesminded people assisted by administrative people with little or no say in major decisions." [107]

Since comparatively new stock companies far outnumber established stock companies, and since this discussion concerns systems rather than individual companies, Mr. Gold's observations constitute a serious indictment of the stock company structure.

Argument No. 4—Dividends are not guaranteed and may never be paid. Projections of current dividend scales are exaggerations and cannot be relied on.

Refutation: To test the validity of projections of current dividends scales, I made a study of twenty-year comparisons of projections against actual results for policies purchased in each year from 1941 through 1950. What was a thirty-five-year-old buyer of a $1,000 whole life policy in each of those years led to expect from a projection of the then current dividend scale over the following twenty years, and what *actual* results did he experience? Surely such comparisons clearly reveal whether or not the buyer was misled.

The chart that follows averages these nineteen mutual companies:

Berkshire	National Life, Vermont
Connecticut Mutual	New England Mutual

---

[107] Ibid.

Equitable (N.Y.)   New York Life
Guardian   Northwestern Mutual
John Hancock   Pacific Mutual
Massachusetts Mutual   Penn Mutual
Metropolitan   Phoenix Mutual
Mutual Benefit   Provident Mutual
Mutual Life (N.Y.)   Prudential
              State Mutual

(These companies were chosen because they are the only mutual companies included in the annual *Flitcraft Courant* review every year of the ten under consideration.)

Twenty-Year Period	Average Annual Net Premium [108] Projected at Start of Period	Average Annual Net Premium [109] Actually Paid
1941–1961	$20.98	$20.55
1942–1962	21.31	20.58
1943–1963	21.48	20.45
1944–1964	21.50	20.33
1945–1965	21.50	20.22
1946–1966	21.47	20.05
1947–1967	21.44	19.87
1948–1968	21.31	18.86
1949–1969	21.39	18.67
1950–1970	21.06	18.48

This analysis involved ten twenty-year periods for each of the nineteen companies, a total of 190 calculations. In only fourteen of these was the actual history less favorable than the projection. The

[108] *Flitcraft Compend,* 1941 through 1950.

[109] *Flitcraft Compend,* 1961 through 1970.

difference against the policyholders (included in the illustrated results) was only 34 cents in the average net annual premium. The
average of those fourteen instances was $20.82 projected, $21.16
actually paid. The other 176 calculations gave the policyholder a
better break than was indicated by the projection of the dividend
scale at the time of his purchase.

Does such a remarkable record justify a charge that dividend projections mislead a prospective buyer?

The most recent comparison of dividends projected and dividends actually paid appeared in *Best's Review* of August 1970. It
covered the ten-year period on $1,000 whole life policies bought in
1961 by men age thirty-five, in sixty-nine companies. The results
showed that only two companies paid less in dividends over the ten
years than their 1961 projections indicated. One of these averaged
49 cents less than the projection; the other, 28 cents less.

Repeatedly, the annual *Flitcraft Courant* study (the Flitcraft
firm has had a reputation for statistical accuracy for many decades)
comparing dividends actually paid with dividends projected at the
time of purchase, opens with these words:

> Dividend illustrations—how valid are they? When a prospect is
> faced with figures on competing policies of two or more companies,
> he wants to know two things if the figures deal with projections:
> —If I buy a policy offered to me, will my actual cost be some-
> where near projected cost?
> —If I take the policy in the company which projects the lower
> cost, will I probably have a lower actual cost than if I did not take
> that particular policy?

The *Flitcraft Courant* answers its two questions, for whole life,
age thirty-five, in the affirmative. "Yes," it says, year after year,
"the prospect can expect that his actual cost will probably be about
what the projection indicates, and if he buys in a company projecting a considerably lower cost than another, his cost will probably be
correspondingly lower."

These conclusions are based on studies of both mutual companies
and the participating policies of stock companies. The fanatical dev-
otees of nonparticipating insurance make no distinction—they sim-

ply hate all dividends and distrust the projections of current dividend scales by both types of companies. Being fanatics, they are uninfluenced by facts. When faced with them in competition, they revert to Argument No. 1—the fallacious results of investing the differences in the guaranteed premiums.

Argument No. 5—"One disadvantage inherent in the participating form which should not go without mention is that it leads too often to selling on a basis of projected net cost; that is, the agent represents to the buyer that the net cost of the insurance over the period of policy will be comparable to, if not identical with the net cost either (1) over a period of past history (10 to 20 years usually) or (2) with what the current dividend scale would make it." [110]

Refutation: In view of the actual histories of dividend payments, and the remarkable accuracy of dividend projections, this contention is little short of fatuous. It would be unrealistic, if not worse, for agents to ignore the basic nature of participating policies, which this argument clearly suggests. Would it enlighten prospective buyers to describe participating policies as if they were nonparticipating?

There is no better illustration of the public's faith in the reliability of dividend projections than the fact that most mutual companies, year after year, sell 40 percent to 50 percent of their new business to their old policyholders.

As far as I can ascertain, there are no other pro-nonparticipating or anti-participating arguments. I suspect they are made to convince or reassure agents. Since actual performance figures are readily available and show beyond doubt that over the years mutual participating policies are far superior to nonparticipating life insurance, strange contentions are essential to attract and retain salesmen for stock companies, and to enable them to sell an unattractive type of life insurance.

---

[110] *Modern Life Insurance,* Mehr and Osler.

Chapter **8** *Conclusion*

Undoubtedly, there are some stock life insurance companies more efficiently managed than some mutuals are. In the cost area, it is possible that a particular stock company may be superior to a particular mutual. But, I remind you, unnecessarily I hope, that I am concerned not with individual companies, but with systems.

My conclusion, that all existing stock life insurance companies be compelled to mutualize and that new ones be prohibited, is based on these beliefs:

—Life insurance cannot be sold at cost when stockholders participate in operational gains. Only the mutual system eliminates profits to stockholders.

—The lure of profits has steered stock company management into holding companies, and other diversifications, that evade restrictions imposed by the regulatory authorities and threaten the soundness of the entire life insurance operation.

—The lure of profits (at the expense of policyholders) has created the unwholesome proliferation of new stock life insurance companies. The demise of many of them has resulted in loss to policyholders and their beneficiaries. Many of those that have thus far survived use questionable methods of obtaining the services of agents, who in turn inevitably face conflicts of interest that lead to reprehensible sales tactics.

—The anomaly of participating life insurance sold by stock companies creates an irreconcilable conflict between stockholders and policyholders.

—To compete with lower-cost participating policies, many of the agents selling nonparticipating life insurance have been compelled to make fallacious sales arguments.

—The money invested by stockholders in established companies is totally unnecessary to company operations and, being riskless, is unworthy of participation in profits.

—New stock companies fulfill no public need. If they fail, policyholders as well as investors are the losers. If they survive, they will be in the same antipublic position now occupied by the established stock companies.[111]

—Mutualization has proved to be in the public interest, and has been accomplished through fair and lawful means.

The instances of corruption that I have cited have all been in the stock ownership field. There has not been a single charge of corruption against any mutual company since the Armstrong Investigation in 1905, and even then the few mutuals under attack were challenged only for business practices common to the era, and not for

---

[111] ". . . huge oil companies and merchandising chains, as well as credit card companies, conglomerate corporations and others are in the life insurance field. . . . They will not hesitate to use means and methods which established life insurance companies would consider to be highly unorthodox." (John W. Popp, partner, Peat, Marwick, Mitchell & Company, highly regarded C.P.A.s quoted by *The National Underwriter*, October 3, 1970.)

actions that produced personal profits for management at the expense of policyholders. Stock companies, on the other hand, because of their very stockholder-oriented foundation, provide a fertile field for the seeds of corruption.

REGULATION IS A VITAL CONSIDERATION

While effective regulation can correct whatever management faults exist in mutual company operation, it is impossible to contend with all the vagaries of stock company management. Regulation has not prevented stock company insolvencies, whether due to incompetence or criminal activity. It has not prevented holding companies that permit stock companies to evade measures enacted in the public interest. Regulation simply cannot contend with what is basically antisocial—profits to stockholders for doing nothing more than the public can do for itself.

Criticism of mutual life insurance companies, even if justifiable, is not pertinent to the issue under consideration. That issue is whether the continued existence of stock life insurance companies is in the public interest. Clearly, it is not.

EFFECTIVE COMPETITION WILL NOT BE REDUCED

Some will contend that the elimination of stock life insurance companies will dangerously reduce the element of competition in the life insurance field. Such a contention has no merit whatever. Back in the mid-forties, when there were fewer than five hundred companies operating, competition among them was intense, and the public was amply protected against monopolistic control. Governmental regulations of various kinds precluded then, and certainly does now, any possibility of it. The entrance into the field of those thousands of new companies since World War II added nothing to the degree of competition. As a matter of fact this was admitted by those new companies. Consider these observations:

> "The lack of size gives us a unit cost much higher than that of the older company . . ." [112]
>
> "Realistically, the usual young company is definitely at a disadvantage in attempting to compete, cost-wise, with its large established competitors." [113]
>
> "New companies admit that they cannot compete with the big established insurers on a rate book basis." [114]

If mutualization were made mandatory, the established stock companies, following the pattern set by the Equitable, the Metropolitan, and the Prudential, would retain their identities, as would a limited number of the newer stock companies. The others would be absorbed by mutuals. It is a certainty that the mutualization program would leave a minimum of five hundred companies operating in America. And that number would be more than ample to guarantee the desired degree of competition, and to serve the needs of the American public.

WILL FEWER COMPANIES BE ABLE TO SERVE THE PUBLIC NEED?

Once a life insurance company (mutual or stock) becomes established, it has an unlimited capacity for doing business. It does not rely on raw materials or machines. It sells a service, not a product. It is true that a growing life insurance company requires increasing manpower (mitigated, of course, by computers) but that is not a problem in view of our expanding population.

---

[112] Phil J. Schwanz, President, Midwestern United Life Insurance Company, Fort Wayne, at the Conference for Young Life Insurance Companies, Chicago, September 2, 1965.

[113] Robert D. Williams, at the Conference for Young Life Insurance Companies, Chicago, September 1, 1965.

[114] Report of *The National Underwriter* on the 1964 Annual National Association of Life Companies meeting, July 25, 1964.

Could five hundred companies effectively serve our population increase? Should we grow to 300 million, we would then have a ratio of one company for every 600,000 people. Japan, with twenty-five companies (twenty-four of them mutuals) has a ratio of one to 4 million; Italy, one to 2 million; France, one to 750,000; Great Britain, one to 400,000.

REGULATION WILL BE MORE EFFECTIVE

The reduction in the number of companies operating in our country would not reduce competition or the ability to serve. It would, moreover, materially increase the effectiveness of regulation, a consummation devoutly to be wished for. Too many companies (our present situation) means ineffective regulation.[115] "There is reason to think American regulators have lost control of the market in the sense that they are not able to keep close enough contact with what is going on to detect incipient difficulty and anticipate failure. The frequency with which questionable practices develop, as well as the common occurrence of actual liquidations, and the higher frequency of mergers and total reinsurance, which often suggest, even when they do not actually prove, that there is difficulty, are eloquent testimony to the inadequate control that American regulators can maintain over the insurance market. They struggle manfully to repair the leaks in the dyke, but they are not able to prevent them.[116]

---

[115] Twenty Illinois life insurers have been warned they face . . . financial difficulties, and have been requested to take certain precautions, according to James Baylor Illinois Insurance Director. (*The National Underwriter,* October 3, 1970)

[116] In its issue of September 12, 1970, *The National Underwriter* quoted Charles D. Mathews, member of the Texas Insurance Board, as having said, "With the tremendous increase in the volume of business done in the field of insurance, and coverage extending into the billions of dollars, more and more concern has been focused on the solvency of companies. This is a matter of utmost concern to the regulator, because we have a duty—an obligation—to see to it that companies writing business are solvent, and equally, if not greater, a duty and obligation to

139

Though such judgment must necessarily be subjective, the author has the impression that many European regulators have materially better command of the situation in their respective countries." [117]

Mutualization, then, would serve many purposes. It would reduce the cost of life insurance for the millions who have thoughtlessly bought stock company life insurance (and those who otherwise might buy it in the future). It would eliminate all possibility of "the barbarities of corporate plunder," [118] and it would, through a drastic reduction in the number of companies operating, make regulation far more effective. In fact, mutualization would be a boon to the American people.

A FINAL COMPARISON

We now know a good deal about unreasonable profits to risk-proof owners of shares in established stock life insurance companies; about holding companies and diversification and conglomerates engineered by stockholders' interests, a few in open conflict with policyholder interests; about new stock company promotions that frequently have ended in bankruptcy, often accompanied by criminal acts. How does it all stack up against this description of a mutual life insurance company, a description endorsed practically unanimously by top mutual managements?

A mutual life insurance company is nothing more than a mechanism for the pooling and subsequent distribution of funds of a group of people, who must provide for the possibility of adversity.

---

protect the consuming public from doing business with shaky and financially unsound companies.

"This problem has become of tremendous importance because of the change in our present economy coupled with the great number of catastrophic losses which have occurred in Texas and elsewhere in the United States in recent weeks and months."

[117] "Sketches from a Comparative Study of American and European Insurance Regulation," Spencer L. Kimball, in the June 1965 issue of *The Journal of Insurance.*

[118] Richard E. Stewart, New York Superintendent of Insurance.

The number one responsibility of the trustees of the company is to make sure that the funds of the members are applied as the members intended. It must never be forgotten that the funds belong to the members and that the officers and trustees do not have any God-given right to use these funds for purposes which appeal to the officers or trustees, but which may be adverse to the best interests of the contributors.[119]

While it is not unanimously accepted that "ours is a society struggling to become cooperative," [120] there can be no doubt about the acceptance of cooperative or mutual life insurance. Despite the fact that stock life insurance companies outnumber the mutuals by more than ten to one,[121] the mutuals have 70 percent of the assets of all United States life insurance companies.[122]

Nevertheless, some will ask, "How can a capitalistic, free enterprise society prohibit stock life insurance companies?" A far more challenging question is: How can a nation that has adopted a graduated income tax, created a monopoly-control system, and effected a multiplicity of welfare and social security benefits permit them?

---

[119] Daniel J. Lyons, Chairman of Guardian Life, in *The National Underwriter,* June 6, 1970.

[120] Rexford Guy Tugwell.

[121] *1970 Life Insurance Fact Book.*

[122] Ibid.

Appendixes

Appendix A

Partial Record of Holding Company Diversifications

The holding companies are printed in capital letters. The companies in which they have at least a 50 percent stock ownership are listed under them, with life insurance companies listed first.

AETNA LIFE AND CASUALTY COMPANY, HARTFORD

Aetna Life Insurance Company
    Excelsior Life Insurance Company
    Participating Annuity Life Insurance Company
    Variable Annuity Sales Company of Conn.
Aetna Casualty and Surety Company
    Span Data Processing Center Inc.
    REI of Arlington Inc.
    West Fort Corp.
    Crocker-Aetna Company
Standard Fire Insurance Company
Automobile Insurance Company
Civil Finance Corporation
    Civic Hampton Corporation
    Civic Western Corporation
    Civic Southern Factors Corporation
    Five Thirty North Water Corporation
    North Hamilton Corporation
Koll Income Properties Inc.

Aetna Fund Inc.
AGEN Holdings Limited
 United Holdings Limited
  Producers and Citizens Fire and General Insurance Company
  Hyde Real Estate Ltd.
  United Holdings Investments
  Lacy Proprietary Ltd.
   Squadron Investments Prop. Ltd.
 Producers and Citizens Life Insurance Company Ltd.
  Producers Properties Ltd.
  Mena House Prop., Ltd.
  Aotearca Property Company, Ltd.
  Associated Properties Ltd.
Aetna Financial Services Inc.
Aetna Investment Management Inc.
Urban Investment and Development Company

AMERICAN FINANCIAL CORP., CINCINNATI

United Liberty Life Insurance Company
Rubenstein Construction
Provident Bank
American Computer Leasing
 American Computer Service Corporation
Hunter Savings Association
American Home Savings Association
Demsey & Siders Ins. Agency

AMERICAN GENERAL INSURANCE COMPANY HOUSTON

American General Life Insurance Company
American General Life Insurance Company of Oklahoma
Hawaiian Life Insurance Company, Ltd.
Patriot Life Insurance Company, N.Y.
Maryland Life Insurance Company of Baltimore
American General Life Insurance Company of N.Y.
Variable Annuity Life Insurance Company
Channing Financial Corporation
 Van Strum & Towne, Inc.
 Channing Co., Inc.
  Emmett A. Larkin Co., Inc.
 Channing Service Corporation
 Chanstat Services, Inc.

146

Knickerbocker Corporation
American General Management Company
American General Life Insurance Company of Delaware
American General Investment Corporation, Texas
    American General Realty Company
    Atlas Realty Company
Fidelity & Deposit Company of Maryland
Life & Casualty Insurance Company of Tennessee
    WLAC Inc. WLAC FM & AM
    Nashville Magazine, Inc.
    WLAC TV
    World-Wide Assurance Company
Title Guarantee Company
American General Equipment Leasing Corporation
Agricultural Livestock Finance Corporation
Maryland Casualty Company
    Northern Insurance Company of N.Y.
        Assurance Company of America
        Maine Bonding and Casualty
    Maryland American General Insurance Company
    National Standard Insurance Company
    Whyburn & Co.
    Robert Hampson & Son, Ltd.
        Weber General Insurance Ltd.
        Gordon Insurance Agencies, Ltd.
    Marcasco Co. Incorporated
    McManus & Co., Inc.

AMERICAN HERITAGE LIFE INVESTMENT CORP.

American Heritage Life Insurance Company
Florida Associated Services, Inc.
Florida Leasing and Financing Co., Inc.
American Century Advisers, Inc.

AMERICAN INSURANCE MANAGEMENT CORP.

Central Reserve Life of North America Insurance Company
Kochler Insurance Association
Ohio Indiana Mutual Investment Corporation
ABCD Corporation

AMERICAN INTERNATIONAL GROUP, INC.

National Union Life Insurance Company of Pittsburgh
American Life Insurance Company
Delaware American Life Insurance Company
American Home Assurance Company
Insurance Company of the State of Pennsylvania
Transatlantic Reinsurance Company
American International Life Assurance Company of N.Y.
Commerce and Industry Insurance Company
National Union Fire Insurance Company
Birmingham Fire Insurance Company of Pennsylvania
Lexington Insurance Company
Hunter Lyon, Inc.
Southwestern General Agency
New Hampshire Insurance Company
American Fidelity Company
Granite State Insurance Company
Illinois National Insurance Company
    Inland National Insurance Company
New Hampshire Company, Inc.
Manchester Insurance Corporation

ASSOCIATED COMPANIES, INC.

Laymen Life Insurance Company
Associated Companies Realty Corporation
Insur-Equity
    Investors Institutional Services, Inc.

ASSOCIATED MADISON COMPANIES, INC.

Madison Life Insurance Company
First Madison Capital Corporation

AVCO CORPORATION

Paul Revere Life Insurance Company
    Paul Revere Variable Annuity Insurance Company
    Paul Revere Equity Sales Company
    Paul Revere Equity Management Company
Avco Broadcasting Corporation
Avco Delta Corporation

Avco Economic Systems Corporation
Avco Embassy Pictures Corporation
Carte Blanche Corporation
Moffats Limited
Paul Revere Corporation
Rancho Bernardo, Inc.
Seaboard Finance Company
Ventura Savings & Loan Association

BANKERS MORTGAGE CORP.

Continental Bankers Life Insurance Company
Ban-Con, Inc.
Bankers Security Corporation
Bankers Title Guaranty

BANKERS UNITED MANAGEMENT CORPORATION

Bankers United Life Assurance Company
Micro Communications, Inc.
Travel Systems International, Ltd.
    Drake Travel Service, Inc.
    Travel Specialists, Inc.
    Christian Heritage Tours, Inc.
    Bon Voyage Travel Service of Canada Ltd.

BENEFICIAL STANDARD CORPORATION

Beneficial Standard Life Insurance Company
    Beneficial National Life
    British Pacific Life
Beneficial Assurance Company
Fidelity Interstate Life
Transit Casualty
    Selective Insurance Company
    Beneficial Investment Company
    Investment Management, Inc.
Beneficial Computer Services, Inc.
Transequity Investors, Inc.
Benfid Realty Company
    Investment Management, Inc.
    Lincoln Rose Company
    Anchorage Shopping Center
    B&B Shopping Center Company

Benfid-Katz Associates
Benfid-Scott Associates
Benfid-Vernon Associates
Brundage Square
Lincoln Square
Santa Coliseum Company
Big Service Corporation
National Investment Management Company
Oxford Plaza Corporation
Kenai Shopping Plaza
Transtate Investors, Inc.
First Mutual Investors, Inc.
(dba Calif. Investors, Inc.)
California Investors Agency
IDS Realty
Big Eye

BUDGET INDUSTRIES INC.

Transnational Life Insurance Company
Budget Finance Plan
Transnational Insurance Company
Budget Financial Corp.
Budget Holding Company
Century Bank
State Savings & Loan Association

CAPITAL FUNDING CORP.

American Pacific Life Insurance Company of California
Capital Securities Corporation
Capital Insurance Associates
R. J. Baker Company
Hackman Dahl & Company
Capital Overseas Corporation

CHUBB CORPORATION

Colonial Life Insurance Company of America
Federal Insurance Company
Pacific Indemnity
Northwestern Pacific Indemnity

Texas Pacific Indemnity
Vigilant
Great Northern
La Fédération Européenne, Compagnie d'Assurance
Premium Credit Corporation
Underwriters Service Corporation
Chubb & Son, Inc.
Federal Business Products, Inc.
Macro Services Corporation

CITY INVESTING COMPANY

Peoples-Home Life
Federal Life & Casualty Company
Westamerica Securities Inc.
Home Insurance Company, N.Y.
Home Indemnity Company
Seaboard Surety Company
THICO Plan, Inc.
THICO Finance, Inc.
Guerdon Industries
Wilson Shipyards
Southern California Savings & Loan
Motel 6, Incorporated
Wells Marine, Inc.
Hayes International Corporation
Rheem Manufacturing Company
World Color Press, Incorporated
C.I. Management Corporation

CNA FINANCIAL CORPORATION

Valley Forge
Continental Assurance Company
Mid-States Life
National Retirement Forum, Inc.
National Fire
Transcontinental
Transcona Corporation
Continental Casualty Company
Transportation Insurance Company
Mid-States Insurance Company
Canada Health & Accident Assurance

CNA Casualty
Concasco Corporation
Surplus Lines, Inc.
American Casualty
    Valley Forge
    ACCO, Inc.
    ACCO Realty Corp.
CNA Administrative Services, Inc.
Joshua B. Glasser Association
Canadian Premier Life
General Finance Company
    Vacations Unlimited, Inc.
    Vacation Tours
CNA Investor Services, Inc.
    Personal Income Plans, Inc.
TSAI Management & Research Corp.
    TSAI Investment Services, Inc.
    TMR, Inc.
    TMR Ventures
    Employees Consultant, Inc.
CNA Realty Corporation
Kane Financial Corporation
    Massachusetts Capitol Corporation
    High Plain Realty Trust
    Garden City Trust
    Downtown Realty Trust
        Village Improvement Trust
        Felluca Realty Trust
    Kane Hyannis Corporation
    Quechee Lakes Corporation
Larwin Group, Inc.
    Larwin Properties Corporation
    Brentwood Mortgage Corporation
    Wilshire National Life Insurance Company
Nuclear Energy Leasing, Inc.
CNA Hotel & Leisure, Inc.

COLONIAL PENN GROUP, INC.

Colonial Penn Life Insurance Company
Intramerica Life Insurance Company
Colonial Penn Insurance Company
Grand Circle Travel

National Association Plans, Inc.
Group Association Plans, Inc.
Colonial Penn Group Data Corporation
Hawthorne Advertising, Inc.
Hawthorne Advertising Services, Inc.
Temporary Employee & Mature Persons Services, Inc.
Mature Temps, Inc.

COLLEGE UNIVERSITY CORPORATION

College Life Insurance Company
    University Life Insurance Company of America
    College Life Development Corporation
College/University Insurance Company
College Park Corporation
    College Park Credit Corporation

CONGENERIC

Sentinel Life Insurance Company
Dyna-Growth Financial
M. E. D. Inc.
Time Fire & Casualty

CONNECTICUT GENERAL INSURANCE CORPORATION

Connecticut General Life Insurance Company
    Puritan Life Insurance Company
Aetna Insurance Company
    Aetna Fire Underwriters,
    Century Indemnity Company

CONTINENTAL CORPORATION

National-Ben Franklin Life Insurance Corporation
National Life Assurance Company, Canada
Insco, Systems Corp.
Capital Finance Corporation
  Capital Finance Affiliates
Marine Office-Appleton & Cox Corporation
    U.S.P. & I. Agency, Inc.
    Marine Office-Appleton & Cox Ltd.
    Global Marine Services
Continental Insurance Company, N.Y.

Fidelity & Casualty, N.Y.
Niagara Fire Insurance Company
Buckeye Union Insurance Company
American Title Insurance Company
Columbia Real Estate Title Insurance Company
Kentucky Bar Title Insurance Company
Texas Title Guaranty Company, Inc.
Title Insurance Corporation of Pennsylvania
Amtitle Trust Company
AFCO Credit Corporation
Agent Service Plan of California
AFCO Acceptance Corporation
Fidelity-Phoenix Ins. Co., N.Y.C.
CAFO Ltd.
Firemen's Insurance
Dominion Insurance Corporation, Canada
Royal General Insurance Company, Canada
Underwriters Adjusting Company
Appleton & Cox, Inc.
Appleton & Cox, Inc.
Illinois Appleton & Cox, Inc.
Commercial, New Jersey
Washington General Insurance Corporation
National-Ben Franklin Insurance
AFCO Agent Service Corporation
Pacific Insurance
Seaboard Fire & Marine
Boston Old Colony
Equitable Fire
Upper Canada Insurance Company
Raymond D. Warner Corporation
Warner and Company
American International Insurance Company
National Reinsurance Corporation
Niagara Insurance
National-Ben Franklin Insurance, Ill.
National-Ben Franklin Insurance, Michigan
Jersey
Glens Falls
Kansas City F. & M
Glenway Corp.
Glenplan Corp.

CONTROL DATA CORPORATION

American Health & Life Insurance, N.Y.
American Health & Life Insurance Company, Baltimore
Farmers & Bankers Life Insurance Company
Commercial Credit Company (Delaware)
American Credit Indemnity Company of New York
Calvert Fire Insurance Company
Cavalier Insurance Corporation
Eastern Insurance
Agar Packing
Cronam Inc.
Goslin Birmingham
Grabler Mfg.
Kaydon Engineering
Kerotest Mfg.
Miller Printing
Shaffer Spring
AFLC Inc.
C C Leasing.
Central Information Processing
City Loan & Savings
Commercial Credit Business Loans
Commercial Credit Corporation, Ltd.
Commercial Credit Equipment Corporation
Commercial Credit Industrial Corporation
Commercial Credit Plan, Inc.
Computer Finance Corp.
International Rediscount Corp.
R.A. Auto Fleet Leasing Ltd.
Textile Banking Co.

DIVERSA, INC

Girard Life Insurance Company of America
Exchange Park Company & Subsidiaries
Murmanill Corporation & Subsidiaries
Apparell Corporation of America

DYNAMIC SECURITY CORP.

Dynamic Security Life Insurance Company
Dynamic Information Systems

155

    Dynamic Security Properties
    Dynamic Securities Corporation

EDUCATOR & EXECUTIVE COMPANY

    Educator & Executive Life Insurance
    Educator & Executive Insurers, Inc.
    Educator & Executive Insurance Agency, Inc.
    E & E Securities, Inc.
    Worth Counsel Corporation
    Ranger Securities Corporation

EMPIRE GENERAL CORP.

    Empire Life, Los Angeles
    Empire Life, Cleveland
    Empire Life, Chicago
    Empire Life Reinsurance Company
    Empire Fund Management Company
    Empire Securities of Ohio
    Empire Computer Services
    Empire Development Corp.
    Empire General

EQUITY FUNDING CORPORATION OF AMERICA

    Presidential Life Insurance Company
    Investors Planning Corporation of America
    Ankony Angus Corporation
    Ankony Hyland Angus, Inc.
    Liberty Savings and Loan Association
    Crown Savings & Loan Association

FIDELITY CORPORATION

    Fidelity Bankers Life Insurance Company
    Northeastern Life Insurance Company of New York
    Concord Life Insurance Company
    Central National Life Insurance Company of Omaha
    Akron Savings & Loan Company
    Fidelity Management Company
    Information Services Company
    Protective Insurance Underwriters, Inc.
    Central National Insurance Company of Omaha

Protective National Insurance Company of Omaha
Security Assurance Company
Halsey Corporation
Fidelity & Guaranty (Continental) Ltd.

GAMBLE SKOGMO, INC., MINNEAPOLIS

Gamble Alden Life Insurance Company
Aldens, Inc.
Gambles Holiday Travel Service
Gambles Continental State Bank
Gamble-Alden Securities Inc.
Red Owl Stores, Inc.
J. M. McDonald Company
Eisen Mercantile Division
Mode O'Day
Rasco Stores Division
Gamble Development Company
Gamble MacLeod Ltd.
Clark's-Gamble of Canada Ltd.

GLOBE CAPITAL CORP.

Loyal American Life Insurance Company
Globe Assurance Company
      Balanced Investment Corporation
      Citizens Universal Life Insurance Company
Datalogics, Inc.
Service Insurance Agency

GREATER OHIO CORP.

Greater Ohio Life Insurance Company
Greater Ohio Casualty Agencies, Inc.
Greater Ohio Realty Company
Greater Ohio Management & Research Corporation
First National Bank, Mt. Gilead, Ohio

GREAT WESTERN LOAN & TRUST CO.

Great Western Life Insurance Company
Great Western Finance Company
Great Western Finance Company of Seguin, Texas

GULF LIFE HOLDING COMPANY

Gulf Life Insurance Company
American Amicable Life Insurance Company
U.S. Life Insurance Company, Waco, Texas
Stonewall Insurance Co.
Gulf Enterprises, Inc.
  Atlantic Discount
  Dependable Insurance Company

GULF & WESTERN INDUSTRIES, INC.

Capitol Life Insurance Company
Associates Corporation of North America
  Emmco Insurance Company
    Excel Insurance Company
      Capco Adjusters, Inc.
  Associates Financial Services Corporation
  Associates Leasing Corporation of Indiana
  Associates Capital Corporation
  First Bank & Trust Company
  Northern Illinois Corporation
  Associates Discount Corporation
  Associates Finance Corporation
  Associates First Discount Corporation
  Associates Acceptance Company Ltd. of Canada
  Providence Washington Insurance Company
  Clemens Metal Products Company, Inc.
Paramount Pictures Corporation
South Puerto Rico Sugar Company
Taylor Forge, Inc.
Unicard, Inc.
Universal American Corporation
Brown Company
Consolidated Cigar Company
Global Systems Inc.
Chicago Thoroughbred Enterprizes Inc.
New Jersey Zinc Company
E. W. Bliss Company
America Parts Company, Inc.

ILLINOIS AGRICULTURAL ASSOCIATION

Country Life Insurance Company

158

ILLINOIS AGRICULTURAL HOLDING COMPANY

Country Mutual Insurance Company
Country Casualty Insurance Company
Mid-America Fire and Marine Insurance Company
Country Capitol Investment Fund, Inc.
Country Capitol Management Company

ILLINOIS MUTUAL LIFE & CASUALTY COMPANY

IMCO CONSOLIDATED, INC.
IMCO Computer Systems Inc.
IMCO Investors, Inc.

INA CORPORATION

Life Insurance Co. of North America
 INA Life Insurance Company of New York
INA Properties
Insurance Company of North America
Pacific Employers Insurance Company
Philadelphia Investment Corporation
Star Sprinkler Corporation

INTEGON CORPORATION

Integon Life Insurance Corporation
Integon General Insurance Corporation
Integon Indemnity Corporation
Integon Investment Management Corporation
Integon Computer Corporation
Integon Realty Corporation
Integon Finance Corporation
Integon Equity Sales Corporation

INTERFINANCIAL, INC.

United Family Life Insurance Company
Union Security Life Insurance Company
American Security Insurance Company
 Standard Guaranty Insurance Company
 Paco, Inc.
International Securities Corporation
 Coordinated Capital Consultants

> Venture Management Company
> International Securities of Canada

INTERSTATE CORP.

> Interstate Life & Accident Insurance Company
> Interstate Fire Insurance Company
> Invesco
> Real Estate Development Corp.

ISC INDUSTRIES

> Old Security Life Insurance Company
> First S.W. Life Insurance Company
> Interstate Securities Company
> Old Security Casualty Insurance Company
> Financial House Insurance Services
> United Security Underwriters Ltd.
> Security Systems, Inc.
> Joseph Lipic Pen Company
> Cline Truck Company
> Hardwick Mfr. Company
> U.S. Forge Craft

JEFFERSON-PILOT CORPORATION

> Jefferson Standard Life Insurance Company
> Pilot Life Insurance Company
> J-P Investments Inc.
> Pilot Fire & Casualty Insurance Company
> Southern Fire & Casualty Company
> Pilot Title Insurance Company
> Jefferson Standard Broadcasting Company
> Jeflerson Standard Broadcasting Company of Virginia
> North Carolina Broadcasting Company

KENTUCKY CENTRAL LIFE INSURANCE COMPANY

MID-CENTRAL INVESTMENT COMPANY, INC.

> Kentucky Central Insurance Company
> Kentucky Central Television, Inc.
> Liberty Securities Corp.
> Cree Management Company, Inc.
> Duck Key, Inc.

Duck Key Properties, Inc.
Indies Inn, Inc.
    Douglas Investment Company, Inc.
Investment Securities Corporation
    Dania Bank
Key Investment Corporation
Foundation Investment Corporation
Hollis Company, Inc.

LEASCO DATA PROCESSING EQUIPMENT CORPORATION

Reliance Standard Life Insurance Company
Reliance Life Insurance Company
Leasco Computer Inc.
Leasco Systems & Research Corporation
Werner Associates, Inc.
Louis Berger Inc.
CTI-Container Transport International, Inc.
Leasco World Trade
National Union Indemnity Company
Reliance Insurance Company
Planet Insurance Company
United Pacific Insurance Company
General Casualty Company of Wisconsin
Cananwill, Inc.
1600 Kennedy Boulevard Corporation
Four Penn Center Building Corporation
Pilot Insurance Company

LIBERTY CORPORATION

Liberty Life Insurance Company
Special Services Corporation
LPC of North Carolina, Inc.
Surety Realty Corp.
Liberty Corporation Foundation
Westchester Mall, Inc.
Houston Plaza, Inc.
LaMarick System of Beauty Culture of Alabama, Inc.
Hampton Insurance Agency, Inc.
Office Investments, Inc.
Liberty Property Corporation of Texas
    Talisman Management Co.

161

Cosmos Broadcasting Corporation
Cosmos Cablevision Corporation
Cox-Cosmos Inc.
LaMarick Beauty System, Inc.
LaMarick System of Beauty Culture of Tennessee, Inc.
LaMarick System of Beauty Culture of Virginia, Inc.

LIBERTY FINANCIAL CORP.

Liberty Financial Life
Liberty Mortgage Insurance Corporation
Liberty Financial Corporation, Leasing
Liberty Financial Corporation, Realty
Liberty Financial Corporation, Insurance
Mortgage Management Group
Mortgage Investment Trust

LINCOLN CONSOLIDATED, INC.

Lincoln Liberty Life Insurance Company
Funds, Inc.
Consolidated Programs, Inc.
Compensation Programs, Inc.
Benjamin Franklin Savings & Loan Association

LINCOLN NATIONAL CORPORATION

Lincoln National Life Insurance Company
Lincoln Philippine Life Insurance Company, Inc.
Lincoln National Life Insurance Company of New York
Washington Life Insurance Company
American States Life Insurance Company
Dominion Life Assurance Company
Dominion-Lincoln Assurance Company Ltd.
Dominion-Lincoln Equity Assurance Company Ltd.
Compagnie De Réassurance Nord-Atlantique
American States Insurance Company
American Economy Insurance Company
American States Insurance Company of Texas
American Union Insurance Company of New York
Preferred Fire Insurance Company
Equipment Investors, Inc.
LNC Development Corporation
LNC Equity Sales Corporation

LNC Investment Management Corporation
Medical Information Service, Inc.
Chicago Title and Trust Company
 Chicago Title and Trust Building Corporation
 Chicago Title Insurance Company
  Chicago Title Insurance Company of Puerto Rico
  General Title Service Corporation
  Formac Realty Company
Johnson County Title Company, Inc.
Land Title Guarantee and Trust Company
 Northern Ohio Title Company
Manor Motel Corporation
Employee Transfer Corporation
Halsey, Stuart & Company, Inc.
Home Funding Company, Inc.
 Chicago Title Company
Hall & McChesney, Inc.
L C Investment Corporation
 Lake County Trust Company
McHenry County Title Company
Record Center Corporation
W. W. Vincent & Company

MARCOR INC.

Montgomery Ward Life Insurance Company
Montgomery Ward & Co., Inc.
Cortron Industries, Inc.
Hydro Conduit Corporation
Montgomery Ward Credit Corporation
M-W Properties Corporation
Montgomery Ward Realty Corporation
Montgomery Ward & Company, Incorporated
 Retirement Trust, New York
 Retirement Trust, Chicago
 Profit Sharing Trust
Monwar Property Corporation
Pioneer Trust & Savings Bank
Standard T Chemical Company, Inc.
Fair, Inc.
Container Corporation of America
 California Container Corporation
Delaware Barrel & Drum Company, Inc.

Heisler Corporation
Mengel Company
Monmouth Container Corporation
Mullery Paper Packaging Corporation
Nashville Corrugated Box Company
O. B. Andrews Corporation
Pioneer Paper Box Corporation
Traver Flexible Packaging Corporation

MONARCH CAPITAL CORPORATION

Monarch Life Insurance Company
    Springfield Life Insurance Company, Inc.
Monarch Securities, Inc.
Monarch Investment Management Corp.
Stockbridge Development Corp.
Middlesex Development Corp.
Forge Development Corp.

MORLAN PACIFIC COMPANY

Yosemite Life Insurance Company
Yosemite Insurance Company
    Great Falls Insurance Company
Alpine Insurance Service
Morris Plan Company of California
Commonwealth Bank
Parmer Wood Company

MOTOR CLUB OF AMERICA

Garden State Life Insurance Company
Motor Club of America Insurance Company
    MCA Insurance Company
    Motor Club F. & C. Company

NATIONAL GENERAL CORPORATION

Great American Life Insurance Company
Great American Insurance Company
Republic Indemnity Insurance Company
American National Fire Insurance Company
First Insurance Company of Hawaii, Ltd.
Constellation Reinsurance Company

Columbia Savings & Loan
Grosset & Dunlap
Bantam Books
N G C Theatre Corporation
Transworld Publishers
National General Productions
National General Pictures
Performance Systems
    Minnie Pearl's Chicken
    Royal Castle Systems
    American Child Centers
Wygod, Weis, Florin

NATIONAL INVESTMENT CORPORATION

Continental Investors Life, Inc.
International Investors Life, Inc.
A.I.L. Securities Company, Inc.
National Finance Company, Inc.

NATIONAL LIBERTY CORPORATION

National Liberty Life Insurance Company
National Home Life Assurance Company
De Moss & Associates, Inc.
National Information Services, Inc.
Valley Forge Associates, Inc.

N C N B CORPORATION CHARLOTTE

Superior Life Insurance Company
Stephenson Finance Company, Inc.
Superior Automobile Insurance Company

NLT CORP.

National Life & Accident Insurance Company
Third National Bank
WSM, Inc.
Intereal Company
NLT Computer Services Corp.

165

N N CORPORATION

N N Investors Life Insurance Company
Executive Computer Systems, Inc.
    Abacus, Inc.
    B. R. Starnes Corporation
    Elite Computer Systems, Inc.
N N Dataforms, Inc.
    Southwest Business Forms, Inc.
Agency Service Bureau Corporation
N N Investment Service, Inc.
Talbot Bird & Company, Inc.
Northwestern National Insurance Company
    Oregon Automobile Insurance Company
    North Pacific Insurance Company
    Pacific Automobile Insurance Company
    Northwestern National Casualty Company
    Universal Insurors Company
    Insurance Management Corporation (NNCMIC)
    American Premier Insurance Company
    H. S. Dotson Company
Arthur Wiesenberger Services Corporation

NORTH AMERICAN CORPORATION

North American Equitable Life Assurance Company
    Brookings International Life Insurance Company
Asset Data Systems, Inc.
Parkview Nursing Home, Inc.
House of Haynsworth Printing

NORTH CENTRAL COMPANY

North Central Life Insurance Company
Maine Fidelity Life Insurance Company
North Central Financial Planning
Wall Street Planning
Wall Street Management

NORTHWESTERN FINANCIAL CORPORATION

Northwestern Security Life Insurance Company
M. & J. Financial Life Insurance Company

166

Southern Standard Life Insurance Company
Northwestern Bank
M. & J. Realty Company
Beacon Insurance Company

OLD REPUBLIC INTERNATIONAL CORPORATION

Old Republic Life Insurance Company, Chicago
Norwood Life Insurance Company
Old Republic Life Insurance Company, N.Y.
R. E. Flannery & Associates
    Purchasers Insurance Plan
        Trinity Insurance Agency, Inc.
Old Republic Insurance Company
    Motorists Beneficial Insurance Company

OLD REPUBLIC INTERNATIONAL CORPORATION

Brummel Brothers
    Jet-Set, Inc.
G. Shannon Grover & Company
    Mobile Home Agency, Inc.
        Kent Services, Inc.
Old Republic Assurance Company

OMNICO, INC.

Washington Life Assurance Company
Majestic Life Insurance Company
Roly Manufacturing Company
Electronic Systems Development, Inc.

PENN PACIFIC CORPORATION

First Penn Pacific Life Insurance Company
Lantz International
Business Administration, Inc.

PENNSYLVANIA LIFE COMPANY

Pennsylvania Life Insurance Company
National Central Life Insurance Company
Mayflower Life Insurance Company of America
Pennsylvania Life Insurance Company

Dixie Associates, Inc.
North Carolina United Associates, Inc.
North Atlantic Insurance Agency, Inc.
United Silver Spring Association, Inc.
M. G. Moskowitz & Company, Inc.
H. & R. Block Financial Services
Glenwood Securities
National Central Service Corporation
Automobile Owners Life Insurance Company
Massachusetts Indemnity & Life Insurance Company
Mayflower Service Corporation
Family Security Insurance Agency, Inc.
Penn Union Agency Inc.
Pennsylvania Funding Programs Inc.
Pennsylvania Securities Company
Pacific Programming Corporation
Western Programming Corporation
Willie Mays Agency Inc.

PIEDMONT MANAGEMENT COMPANY INC.

Piedmont Life Insurance Company
Piedmont National Life Insurance Company
Georgia International Life
Reinsurance Corporation of New York
New York Reinsurance Corporation, London
Piedmont Equities Corporation
Piedmont International Ltd.
Lexington Management Corporation
    Renfield Association Services, Inc.
      Lexington Income Managers Inc., Advisor To
        Lexington Income Trust
Templeton Dobbrow & Vance Inc.
Lexington Security Managers Inc.
    Renyx Field & Company
      Corporate Lenders of America Inc., sponsor or advisers to:
        Lexington Corporate Lenders Inc.
        Lexington Research Fund
        Lexington Growth Fund Inc.
        Research Investing Plan
        Mana 1969 Drilling Fund
Vantage Advisors Inc., sponsors of:
    Vantage 1090 Fund

168

PINEHURST CORPORATION, Los Angeles

Founders Life Insurance Company, Los Angeles
    Western Guaranty Life Insurance Company
Pinehurst Financial, Inc.
    Emett & Chandler
    Emett, Chandler & Steven
    Ron Stever & Company
    Commonwealth Assurance Company
    Republic Management Company
    Risk Management, Inc.

PIONEER WESTERN CORPORATION

Western Reserve Life Assurance Company
Fund Research and Management, Inc.
Western Reserve Financial Services Corporation
Computer Assistance Corporation
Franchised Services, Inc.
Balanced Programs, Inc.
Equity Planning Systems, Inc.

PROGRESSIVE CORPORATION

Progressive National Life Insurance Company
Progressive Casualty Insurance Company
Progressive Data Management Corporation
Progressive Premium Budget, Inc.
Lakeside Insurance Agency
Progressive Insurance Agency

PROVIDERS BENEFIT CO.

Providers Benefit Life Insurance Company
Providers Benefit Insurance Company
Providers Benefit Real Estate & Development Company
Providers Benefit Franchise Sales Company
American Providers Diversified, Inc.

REPUBLIC FRANKLIN INCORPORATED

Republic-Franklin Life Insurance Company
Republic-Franklin Insurance Company

RFI Securities
Retirement Systems, Inc.

SAFECO CORPORATION

Safeco Life Insurance Company
General Insurance Company of America
Safeco Insurance Company of America
First National Insurance Company of America
GSL Corporation (Wash.)
General America Corporation (Wash.)
Safeco Credit Company, Inc. (Wash.)
Safecare Company, Inc. (Wash.)
Safeco Securities, Inc.
    Syncro Growth Fund, Inc. (Wash.)
    Syncro Income Fund, Inc. (Wash.)
Land Title Insurance Company (Calif.)
Security Title Insurance Company (Calif.)
    Los Angeles Escrow Company (Calif.)
    Land Escrow & Safe Deposit Company (Calif.)
    Southern California Escrow Company (Calif.)
    California Escrow Company (Calif.)
    Security Title Insurance Company of Washington
        San Juan Title Company (Wash.)
        Bellingham Title Company (Wash.)
        Title Guaranty Company of Grant County (Wash.)
        Title Guaranty Company (Wash.)
            Adams County Title Company (Wash.)
        Land Title Company of Clark County (Wash.)

ST. PAUL COMPANIES, INC.

Western Life Insurance Company
St. Paul Fire & Marine Insurance Company
St. Paul Mercury
St. Paul Title Insurance Corporation
Postal Finance Company
Imperial Financial Services, Inc.
Automated Data Services, Inc.
St. Paul Leasing Co.
Form 1040
Imperial Investment Management Company
Burton Abstract and Title Company

170

SELECTED INVESTMENT CORPORATION

Royal Oak Life Insurance Company
White Whale Restaurants

SILVEY CORPORATION

New American Life Insurance Company
Jefferson Life Insurance Company
Farm & Home Insurance Company
Tri-State Insurance Company
    Farmers & Merchants Insurance Company
    Midwestern Insurance Company
KIM Management & Investment Company, Inc.
Farmers Stock Bank

SOUTHWESTERN GROUP, INC.

Southwestern Security Life Insurance Company
Southwestern Insurance Company
National Discount Insurance Company
Automobile Dealers Insurance Company
Statistical Computor Center

SOUTHWESTERN INVESTMENT COMPANY

Western National Life Insurance Company
Commercial Insurance Company
Midland Empire Insurance Company
Wesco Insurance Company
Bank of Fountain Valley
First Industrial Bank of Colorado Springs
Fountain Valley Insurance Agency, Inc.
Standard Management Company
Standard Leasing Company
Southwest Acceptance Company
Independent Adjustment Company
Standard Improvement Company

TRANSAMERICA CORPORATION

Occidental Life Insurance Company
    American Life Insurance Company
    Transamerica Life Insurance Company

Pacific Fidelity Life Insurance Company
    Countrywide Life Insurance Company
Automotive Insurance Company
Mt. Beacon Insurance Company
Olympic Insurance Company
    Marathon Insurance Company
    Countrywide Insurance Company
Transamerica Insurance Company
    Premier Insurance Company
    Canadian Surety Company
    Surety Fire Insurance Company
    Wolverine Insurance Company
        Riverside Insurance Company
        Secured Development Company
Transamerica Title Insurance Company
Budget Rent-A-Car
Coast Acceptance Company
Coast Service Company
Compagnie Européenne de Banque
De Laval Turbine, Inc.
Foreign Study League
Inter-America
Leisure Corp.
Mortgage Corporation of America
New Corporation
Trans International Airlines
Trans International Hotel Company
Transamerica Computer Company
Transamerica Corporation
Transamerica Financial Corporation
Transamerica Fund Management Company
Transamerica Investment Counselors
Transamerica International Ltd.
Transamerica Land Capital
Transamerica Research Corporation
United Artists Corporation
Transamerica Development Company

TRAVELERS CORPORATION

Caribbean Atlantic Life Insurance Company, Ltd.
Travelers Life Insurance Company, Hartford
Travelers Indemnity Company, Hartford

Charter Oak Fire Insurance Company, Hartford
Travelers Auto Body Company
Reliance Insurance Company of Canada
Phoenix Insurance Company
Equitable Fire & Marine Insurance Company
Standard National Insurance Company
Travelers Insurance Company
Broadcast Plaza, Inc.
Travelers Equities Sales, Inc.
Travelers Investment Management Company
Massachusetts Company, Inc.
Massachusetts Company Distributor, Inc.
Independence Corporation
Prospect Company
Travcom, Inc.
Travelers Research Corporation
Randolph Computer Corp.

UNITED INTERNATIONAL CORP.

Continental Life Insurance Company, Fort Worth, Texas
United Savings Life Insurance Company
Univest Life Insurance Company
Transport Life Insurance Company
United Capital Corporation
Wilkinson Printing Company of Dallas
United Systems International
International Learning Systems

UNIVERSITY COMPUTING COMPANY

Gulf Atlantic Life Insurance Company
Western Security Life Insurance Company
UCC Financial Corporation
Gulf Computer Services, Inc.
Rives, Massey and Hedges
Gulf Insurance Company
Atlantic Insurance Company
Select Insurance Company
Western Credit Corporation

USLIFE CORPORATION

United States Life Insurance Company
South Coast Life Insurance Company

Commonwealth Independence Life Insurance Company
Reliance Life Insurance Company of Illinois
Great National Life Insurance Company
Northwestern Life Insurance Company
Distributors Group Inc.
125 Equity Corp.
Protective Equities Corporation
Mid Services Corp.
South Coast General Insurance Agency Corporation
Inter-County Title
City Finance Company, Inc.
Commerce Company

VANGUARD INTERNATIONAL

California Life Insurance Company
First State Bank
Vanguard Equities
Associated Linen

The above list was compiled from *Corporate Relationships—Insurance Affiliations I*, a *National Underwriter* Publication. That book lists 267 "relationships," of which 160 include life insurance companies. The total list is admittedly incomplete, for the publisher explains that "it does not include all insurance companies, but merely a select list that has become involved in recent years with an organization that deals with other than the insurance business." Moreover, the 267 "relationships" listed "exclude any ownership or control that amounts to less than 50 per cent stock ownership in a particular company."

Appendix B

In recent years, *Best's Review* has published annually a list of stock life insurance company disappearances. The following is a ten year record:

During the Year	Number of Companies "Retired" *
1960	89
1961	83
1962	86
1963	69
1964	90
1965	75
1966	93
1967	83
1968	81
1969	73
	822

* The word "retired" seems to be euphemistic, for the individual reasons for disappearance include: "placed in receivership," "merged into," "reinsured by," "certificate of authority canceled," "assets acquired by," "voluntarily dissolved," "placed in liquidation," "placed in temporary receivership," "dissolved," and "converted to a general business."

Index